The RoMANtic's Guide

"It's the everyday things he does that make Webb a real Romeo."
—*LA Parent*

"Call Michael Webb the master of romance."
—*Dallas Morning News*

"The Martha Stewart of romance."   —*Bozeman Daily Chronicle*

"Men, you slimy reptiles, you. You buy us candy and flowers for Valentine's Day. You take us out to dinner on our anniversary. Well, bad news, guys. A fellow named Michael Webb is making you look bad."   —*Champaign-Urbana News Gazette*

"He's discovered the secrets to keeping passion alive. They go beyond the ordinary shtick of sending flowers or buying candy."
—*Houston Chronicle*

"For the World's Most Romantic Man, Valentine's Day is—quite frankly—amateur night."   —*St. Petersburg Times*

"An authority on romance."   —*New Man Magazine*

"Women want romance, and Michael Webb knows how to give it to them."   —*Quincy Herald-Whig*

"Meet the most romantic husband in America. If you think men have a hard time showing their lovey-dovey side, you haven't met Michael Webb. He's so good at it, he actually teaches other guys!"   —*Woman's World*

"Is this guy for real? He is! He is!"   —*Bridal Guide*

"Sorry ladies, this gem of a husband is reserved for a long, long time."   —*The Sunday Portland Oregonian*

"Want to become the man of every woman's wildest fantasy? Well, all you gotta do is subscribe to *The RoMANtic*."
—*Chicago Daily Herald*

"You should listen to Webb on romance the way you'd listen to Mark McGwire on hitting a baseball."   —*Rocky Mountain News*

The RoMANtic's Guide

HUNDREDS OF CREATIVE TIPS FOR A LIFETIME OF LOVE

MICHAEL WEBB

HYPERION
NEW YORK

Illustrations © Michael J. Mencimer
Book design by Fritz Metsch

Library of Congress Cataloging-in-Publication Data

Webb, Michael
    The RoMANtic's guide : hundreds of creative tips for a lifetime of
love / by Michael Webb — 1st ed.
        p.   cm.
        1. Man-woman relationships—Miscellanea. 2. Love—Miscellanea.
3. Marriage—Miscellanea. I. Title.
HQ801.W55   1999
646.7'8—dc21   99-20475
                                                                    CIP

ISBN: 0-7868-8434-7

FIRST EDITION

10 9 8 7 6

To my precious wife for being so easy to love,
and to a very loving God for sharing her with me.

A Special Thank You

I thank the very special women in my life—wife, mom, sisters, and Aunt Kathy—who taught me much about the more beautiful half and encouraged me to teach others.

I am so thankful for the encouragement, support, and fine skills of my editor, Jennifer Lang, who wholeheartedly believed in my mission from the first day she discovered me. This first book was a joy, thanks to her.

Thanks to my friend and illustrator, Michael Mencimer, who put much energy and devotion into capturing the whimsy and essence of the essays. I love how he hid all those A's (for "Athena") and ♥'s into the drawings. See how many you can find.

Introduction

I never dreamed of writing a book. That simply wasn't on my list of lifelong accomplishments. However, being the best husband on the face of the earth was a goal of mine since I was a teenager.

I grew up surrounded by six sisters and with a mother who suffered through two unhappy marriages. I knew quite a bit about women. I especially knew how easy it was to hurt them.

When I was about sixteen my mom gave me some advice that changed my life. She explained that women weren't really expecting to marry a prince, but they needed two simple things from the man in their life: to be told frequently they are loved and to be shown often they are special.

When I met my wife, Athena, I put into practice my mother's advice. It was difficult and awkward at first, as I'd never seen firsthand a husband truly loving his wife. All my sisters' relationships were as equally unloving (and often more so) as my mom's.

It didn't take long for me to see that romance really did make all the difference, so I began practicing it on a daily basis. With my romantic gestures, Athena was perpetually happy and tried to give back to me more than I would give to her. Seeing how Athena and I were always blissful and never fighting, friends and coworkers began approaching me, asking if I would share some of my romantic ideas with their husbands or boyfriends.

I began publishing *The RoMANtic Newsletter: Hundreds of Fun & Creative Tips on Enriching Your Relationship* and with its instant worldwide success it became my full-time profession. Many subscribers would order every issue I ever produced. They couldn't get enough. I decided to take my best ideas and compile them into this volume of romantic tips. I added a number of my favorite essays from romantics around the globe who contributed their novel ideas to the newsletter.

I doubt if I am indeed the "World's Most Romantic Man" as I am often called, but I still aim to be the world's best husband by telling my wife daily that I love her and showing her often how special she is.

Preface

WHAT IS ROMANCE?

Romance is not a once- or twice-a-year thing. It's not reserved for special occasions, holidays, or just to get out of the "dog house."

Contrary to what many other "romance" books state, romance has little to do with jewelry, chocolates, roses, or sex. Romance doesn't have to be expensive or sap hours from your day.

Man (or woman) is the center of real RoMANce. It's about sharing and giving of yourself. It's a combination of all the little (and big) things you do to say "I love you" and to let someone know how special they are. What is most romantic comes from your heart (and is created by your hands), not from inside your wallet.

Make it a goal to be romantic all year round—starting today.

The RoMANtic's Guide

The Sniffle Stifler

When winter begins to fade away we know the joys (and perils) of spring will soon be here. Fortunately, I do not suffer from allergies but I know hundreds of people who do. They are plagued with swollen eyes, red-tipped noses, and frequent sneezes.

If your sweetheart is battling the sniffles, whether it be from a cold or pollen, this is an opportune time to give a little extra love.

Athena has her own tissue box on her side of the bed. It didn't take me long to disassemble the box and remove a handful of tissues. I wrote encouraging, uplifting, and somewhat silly messages on several of them and returned them to the box. I glued the box back together in no time. Within a week Athena had discovered what I had done. When she pulled out that first message, instantly she forgot whatever pain she was feeling—and simply felt loved.

Laughter might be good medicine but if you combine humor with love, you have an even more potent cure.

The Snow Plan

The snow was falling at a steady rate and I knew the lawn and trees would soon be white. I racked my brain trying to think of a new way to be creatively romantic.

For as long as I tried, nothing clever would come to mind. I peered out the window into our backyard and marveled at how snow blanketed everything in its path. Then I noticed a perfect rectangle of bare ground underneath the backyard bench.

The brilliant idea came to me. The romantic idea didn't have to do with the snow, but the absence of snow. I decided that while it was already too late for this snowfall, I could prepare my romantic ammunition for the next.

The simplest way to execute this plan is to take three large pieces of posterboard or cardboard and with a utility blade or X-Acto knife, cut out I, ♥, and U. Of course you can create as elaborate a message as you have the time, material, and patience. Place the pieces out on the lawn before you are expecting a snowfall or a heavy frost. Hopefully it can be done in the dark of night and then removed early in the morning before your sweetheart awakes. Be sure to cover over your trail to the scene of the crime. When your loved one wakes up, she will see the message in all its splendor.

Trimming the Tiny Tree

So
much
thought is
put into what
gift goes *under* the
Christmas tree for your
love. Have you ever thought
about giving your present *on* the
tree? First, you have to have the right
tree.

A miniature potted Christmas tree makes a perfect gift for the boyfriend or girlfriend who doesn't have the time, money, or desire to drag a full-size tree into their home. For those who already have their "daddy" tree, this "baby" tree is a perfect companion—perhaps even to brighten up a different room of the house or to bring cheer to the office.

Now here is where you can get ultracreative. Sure, you can decorate the tiny tree just like you would do a big one, but you would be missing a grand opportunity.

Consider these clever ways of trimming the midget tree:

- ◆ *For the pet lover*: Decorate with doggy bones, squeaky toys, pet collars, and a leash as a garland.
- ◆ *For the tool-loving guy*: Hang nuts and bolts, small tools like screwdrivers and pliers, and for a garland use a tape measure or a chain.
- ◆ *For the jewelry-loving woman*: Adorn the tree with earrings,

bracelets, and other accessories, and a gold chain or long scarf for the garland.

◆ *For the person with a sweet tooth*: Tie all sorts of candies all over the tree and use strings of licorice for the garland.

That Time of the Month

Marriage, one of the most important events in a person's life, can not be properly celebrated only once a year. It should be cherished daily and celebrated as often as possible. I try to informally celebrate our wedding anniversary on the twenty-seventh of each month (my wife and I were married on May 27).

I don't always plan something elaborate. In fact, sometimes I only buy or make a card for her. It is nearly always a surprise what I plan so she doesn't know if she will receive a card or actually be taken out for a date.

If there is a movie or concert she has been wanting to go to, I buy tickets for that. Or I take her to see a garden or museum on the weekend when we have more time to enjoy it. You don't have to be locked in on celebrating your wedding (or engagement or other special day) a certain day each month. Just try to celebrate it often and with creativity.

WAYS TO CELEBRATE A MONTHLY ANNIVERSARY
◆ Buy or make a card
◆ Visit the zoo or museum
◆ Plan a picnic
◆ Go for a drive through the countryside
◆ See a concert or play
◆ Go out for a special (not necessarily expensive) dinner
◆ Order dinner in and drink champagne
◆ Go to the drive-in

Twelve Romantic Days of Christmas

Forget the swans a'swimming and the partridge in a pear tree. Use ideas from this book to celebrate a creatively romantic Christmas. I guarantee these items are much easier to find than turtle doves and less expensive than golden rings.

On the *first* day of Christmas . . . Buy your mate *one* box of their favorite cereal and lace it with lots of "prizes." Throw in some golf tees, Hershey's kisses, toy cars, or whatever would bring out the child in them.

On the *second* day of Christmas . . . take out your *two* engraved toasting glasses from the china cabinet and use them. Reminisce about the day you first sipped from them. If you don't have any, engrave your own by buying some stencils and etching paste at a crafts store.

On the *third* day of Christmas . . . have *three* meals together. You could go all out with breakfast in bed, a picnic lunch, and a candlelit dinner. Better yet, spend less time preparing the meal and more time sharing it together.

On the *fourth* day of Christmas . . . put the pedal to the metal and *four* on the floor. Take a peaceful drive for the day. Go to the country, sightsee in the city, or cruise around looking at Christmas lights.

On the *fifth* day of Christmas . . . fax or deliver a photocopy of your *five* fingers (plus the rest of your hand) to your love at work. Tell them you can't wait to be together to hold the real thing.

On the *sixth* day of Christmas . . . give her a *half dozen* of her favorite flower—one at a time. Leave one on the pillow, one on her car seat, one at her office, etc.

On the *seventh* day of Christmas . . . count your lucky stars by gazing into the *seventh* heaven. If the night is overcast, arrange glow-in-the-dark ones on the bedroom ceiling.

On the *eighth* day of Christmas . . . buy an *eight*-pack of crayons and together design and color a personalized coloring book of happy memories you have shared.

On the *ninth* day of Christmas . . . cats aren't the only ones with *nine* lives. Take out your scrapbooks, photo albums, or home movies and spend the day soaking up the sweet memories of your past lives together (adolescent, teenager, dating, engaged, married, parent) and then begin planning for the future ones (empty nest, grandparent, retirement).

On the *tenth* day of Christmas . . . massage your sweetheart's aching shoulders for *ten* minutes. Throw in a back scratch, a foot massage, and a hair brushing if you are feeling extra generous.

On the *eleventh* day of Christmas . . . bake *eleven* of your love's favorite cookies (since most recipes make one dozen, these will be bigger than usual—your love won't complain). Stick a wooden skewer through the side of each cookie and then wrap the cookie in a colored plastic wrap. Place them in a box or vase as you would a dozen roses.

On the *twelfth* day of Christmas . . . present your sweetheart with a custom-made *twelve*-month calendar for the new year. Use personal photographs or your own drawings to make it unique. Highlight special days for the new year.

Snow and Ice

I can't think of many more romantic things than snow and ice. Granted, it doesn't snow everywhere in the world, but nearly all major cities sport at least an ice-skating rink, albeit indoors.

Growing up in Louisiana and Southern California, I haven't yet gotten burned out on snow. It doesn't even snow here in North Carolina every year. But when it does,

I've got my mittens on and am ready to go play in it with Athena.

We have the expected snowball fights and build snow people together. We find fresh snow and make homemade snow cones. We go sledding with whatever material we can find. Last year we used a cardboard box, which worked rather well.

Perhaps the best part of the snow is getting out of it. We go inside and sip hot chocolate together while snuggling in front of the fireplace, warming our freezing toes.

The Gift Tree

How
many times
have you heard
a woman say, "It's the
little things that are important"?
This following idea capitalizes on the
concept that it is often better to give ten gifts
valued at ten dollars than to give one gift valued at two
hundred
dollars.

I like to call this idea the gift tree. First you need to go to a stationery, party supply, or gift store and purchase several empty gift boxes in different sizes that can be stacked upon one another. The largest, of course, is at the bottom and the boxes get smaller as you stack them. It is best to stick with the same-shaped boxes whether they're round, square, oblong, or rectangular. The real trick now is to find something small yet meaningful to put in each of the boxes. Perhaps your sweetheart is a chocoholic? Different types of chocolate bars, truffles, or candies could be placed in each box. Maybe they are a sports nut? Fill the boxes with bas-ketball tickets, a cap with their favorite team on it, a packet of trading cards, a baseball, and other paraphernalia. You could do the same for someone with interests in traveling, music, computers, fashion, or even dinosaurs.

Buy a large ribbon, wrap it under the base, and tie it into a bow at the top of the stack. You could get really creative for Christmas and wrap some twinkle lights around the "tree." Whether you allow the "giftee" to open all of the boxes at once or make them wait minutes, hours, or days between the boxes is your call.

Making New Year's Unforgettable

For nearly everyone, January 1 is a day off from work. We often need it, as we are up late the night before "ringing in the New Year."

So the first day of the year is a time to sleep in. And what do I associate with sleeping in? Breakfast in bed!

Now this isn't your ordinary breakfast. This is one served by Baby New Year himself (or herself). For this, you will need to buy or make a Baby New Year costume complete with diaper and sash. If you ever desired to be in a beauty pageant, but never got the chance, now is the opportunity to strut your stuff.

If you have baby cutlery and plates around, you can con-tinue the Baby New Year theme or you can prepare an el-egant breakfast in bed without even having to turn on the stove (see page 30).

One thing is for certain. This would be a New Year's Day that will never be forgotten.

It's Not Full of Hot Air

Are you trying to get someone's attention? Do you want to ask someone out on a date or tell them you love them? Try out this idea.

Take a helium balloon and write your message on two sides with a fat marker (since the balloon is likely to twist around). Take the balloon to their office or home and float it up to the window where they are most likely to see it. It will really impress them if they work on the third or fourth floor. Bet you get that date!

This is also a perfect idea in case you are ever in the position where you need to say "I'm sorry."

I Don't Do Valentines

I do not buy my wife flowers or candy for Valentine's Day or take her out to eat. In fact, I do not do anything special on that day. That may sound ironic, since I claim to be a romantic person. In fact, I think the opposite is true. I don't consider it especially romantic if one does nice things for the love in their life because they feel obligated. If you feel that there is only one day out of the year (or several, if you want to include Christmas, Easter, New Year's, etc.) that you should plan a romantic occasion, you are missing the picture. The romantic traditions of these holidays were probably created by women because these were the only times of the year the men in their lives would do anything special for them.

Every day is a potential day to do something special for the one you love. I would not recommend "forgetting" Valentine's Day if you are not already being actively romantic year-round, but if you are looking for unique days to surprise your wife or girlfriend, try to celebrate on other days—that would show you put a lot of thought into it. Here are some suggestions for nontraditional holidays:

* Month or year anniversary of your first date
* One-month anniversary of her new job
* Six months after her birthday (six months until her next)
* First day of spring
* After passing that big test
* On the birthday of one of your children (she went through a lot to bring that baby into the world)
* Longest day of the year (June 20)

Valentines Worth Sending

If you are going to celebrate Valentine's Day, I suggest you do it with a little forethought. I cringe every time I go to the grocery on February 13 or 14 and see dozens of men crowding around the greeting cards to buy one at the last possible moment.

Buy your card in advance and mail it out to Loveland, Colorado, for extra-special treatment. Your card will be postmarked LOVEland, Colorado, and it will also be hand-stamped with a unique four-line poem.

The Loveland Chamber of Commerce organizes this

yearly romance project with cards going to all fifty states and over one hundred foreign countries annually.

It's simple. Just enclose your preaddressed, prestamped Valentine's card in a larger envelope and mail to: Postmaster, Attn: Valentines, Loveland, CO 80537.

Go ahead. Do it now.

Here are some more "romantic" cities:

♦ Kissimmee, Florida 32741
♦ Valentine, Texas 79854
♦ Valentine, Nebraska 69201
♦ Loving, New Mexico 88256
♦ Bridal Veil, Oregon 97010
♦ Romance, Arkansas 72136

Write On, Wipe Off

For decades men and women have been writing messages on bathroom mirrors. With the invention of dry-erase markers, bathroom mirror communication can be taken to the next level.

A packet of dry-erase markers can be purchased at any office supply store and only cost a couple of dollars. They make great tools with which to pen your sonnets and love notes on mirrors, car windows, and even some appliances.

With a variety of colors you can draw all sorts of pictures on the glass or metal canvas. Decorate the mirror with hearts, smiley faces, or an impressionistic landscape. You could even play tic-tac-toe or hangman.

Best of all, they clean up quickly with a swipe of tissue.

Romance on the Clearance Tables

Sometimes around February, all the calendars that haven't been sold are put on clearance. Many of the calendars like my favorite, the cartoon *The Far Side*, have many more uses than for counting down the days.

Several times I have bought calendars on clearance to add to my "romantic arsenal" (see What Weapons Are You Hiding? on page 138) for future use. Many have funny comics or interesting quotes that make wonderful filler material for all the notes and cards I continually send to my wife.

365-day calendars can be cut up and made into a collage or giant card. Some people use them to create a scrapbook to reflect on the past year. Imagine if you had one of those calendars and wrote down one thing you and your love did on each day and gave it to them for a Christmas or New Year's present at the end of the year.

If you have access to a computer scanner or fax, you might be able to write a personal note on each day and send it to your love at work for a good-morning greeting.

The larger, more colorful calendars make great wrapping paper or can be used to decorate handmade gifts like hat boxes and even "romantic arsenal" boxes.

Put Your Love in Lights

Winter is the perfect time to express your love with lights.

Twinkle lights can be arranged to form messages on roofs, fences, or even on the ground to be seen from above (from a plane, office building, or even a second-story window).

Whether you use the messages to make a marriage proposal or to reaffirm your love, it will certainly make for a very beautiful and memorable evening.

He Plan, She Plan, We Plan

Before our first anniversary, my wife and I decided that we would take turns planning our yearly celebration. We agreed on a budget, but other than that, we each had free reign over planning the annual event. We also determined that every third year we would plan the anniversary jointly and spend a little more and go somewhere our typical budget would not afford. On the years we are planning the anniversary alone, we try to keep the details secret until a few days before the event. Of course, if it involves time off from work, we each let the other arrange those days off in advance.

Because our anniversary nearly always falls on Memorial Day weekend, we get to plan for at least a three-day celebration. Usually, we are able to get away for the entire time, but if not, we plan to do something special each day during that long weekend. After all, it is not only the anniversary of our wedding day, but also of our honeymoon.

If your anniversary is getting to be like a tired cliché, add some spark to it by taking turns planning a creative, romantic, and fun-filled marriage celebration.

In Sickness and In Health

Can you think of a better time to show extra attention to your sweetheart than when she (or he) is sick? One item that is guaranteed to lift anyone's spirits is a get-well basket. Sure, anyone can go to the store and buy a get-well card, but it takes a special person to assemble a get-well basket for the one they love.

You can use practically anything for a "basket." A decorative bowl, a watering can, a candy dish, or any item you can find or buy to put the items in. If you want to go a step beyond, you can decorate the "basket" with balloons, streamers, ribbons, cut-out hearts, or whatever might bring a little extra cheer. Below is a list of possible items you can put in your get-well basket that will have your sweetheart feeling better immediately.

- Get-well card (perhaps handmade)
- Some flowers (from the garden or florist)
- Magazine(s) they like
- New book
- Some tea bags or gourmet coffee
- Fresh lemon and a small jar of honey (help soothe a sore throat)
- Fresh fruit
- Rag doll for her (trust me)
- Stuffed animal
- Doctored-up box of tissues (see The Sniffle Stifler on page 1)

Three Wise Gifts for Christmas

Philip Haney
Decatur, GA

About ten years ago I worked in the country of Yemen, near Saudi Arabia. After two months it was almost time to return home, and I had been thinking for several days about what I could get my wife for a present. Plus, it was near Christmas, so I wanted to find her something that would be really special.

As it turned out, the Christmas story became the key to what I decided to get for her. There we were in a Suburban, bumping along in a wadi (dry streambed) toward a remote farm, when it hit me—I'm in the land of the Queen of Sheba . . . the land of gold, frankincense, and myrrh! That's what I'll give her for a present!

Now I was really motivated.

I looked up the word for frankincense in the Arabic dictionary (*bakor*) and headed for the souk (marketplace) in Taiz, a town in the southern part of the country, not too far from Aden. One of my Yemeni counterparts came with me to help. We both looked and looked until, at last, we found a shop that sold both frankincense and myrrh.

The shop was full of exotic, pleasant aromas and was stuffed with bags of fragrant spices. The shopkeeper measured out about two cups of frankincense and two more of myrrh, wrapped them in plain newspaper, then put the bundles in a plastic carry sack.

Suddenly, I realized that I would need something nice to put the presents in, so we started looking around until we finally found the perfect thing—three shiny brass bowls from India with threaded lids. Now, only one more present remained to be found—the gold.

The next day we went to the gold market in San'a, the ancient capital of Yemen, where gold jewelry is sold by weight. Again, I looked and looked for just the right thing, until I found her a beautiful, delicate necklace. Lovely and very unique, just like her. I was so excited, I could hardly wait to give the gifts to her.

I put everything inside the brass bowls, wrapped them up in the newspaper, and packed them away for the trip back home.

On Christmas day, I casually read the story of the Wise Men who presented Jesus with gifts of gold, frankincense, and myrrh, then gave the three packages to Francesca, wrapped up in the same plain Arabic-language newspaper that the shopkeeper had used. She unwrapped the first one, then the second, and then the third one. The brass bowls were bright and shiny, and seemed even more so in contrast to the plain newspaper, but she hadn't quite realized that there might be something more inside each one.

So I told her, "Go ahead and open them," and she did. First she opened the one with frankincense, which smelled wonderful, then she opened the one with myrrh. At this point she realized that the last one might have something made of gold inside, so she slowly opened it, and found the beautiful necklace inside. It was made of pure gold, and to this day she still considers it one of the most beautiful gifts I have ever given her. Beautiful not only because of its appearance, but because of the story and the thought behind it.

In Love with the Mailman

Who doesn't like the mailman? Well, maybe we all despise him on the days we get a fistful of bills and a pile of junk mail. But other than that, he (or she) brings us some pretty nice stuff. It is fairly easy to send your sweetheart a postcard or letter in the mail. What takes a little more planning and is sure to take their breath away is to mail them a postcard or letter to the location where you will be vacationing or visiting family. I have sent my wife postcards to both my parents' house and her parents' house when we were going to be visiting for a few days. Not only did it bring a smile to her face, it also was a surprise for our parents when they checked the mail. It reinforced in their minds that I was being a loving, devoted husband. Of course that wasn't the reason I sent the postcards, but it was a nice benefit.

You don't have to limit yourself to a postcard. Letters, packages, and priority parcels would make any mate quiver with anticipation. The more thought and preparation you put into it, the greater the thrill will be.

The next time you want to impress your soulmate (or the in-laws), mail a letter to your next destination. It'll be there, rain or shine.

How to Create the Perfect Restaurant

Have you ever been to a progressive dinner? Athena and I have attended a few. It is where you have appetizers at one friend's house, soup at another, then salad, the main course at the fourth, and finally dessert at the last friend's home. It's a great way to taste the various cuisines all the hosts create.

Do you have a favorite restaurant for desserts? How

about one that makes an out-of-this-world soup? Add a few of your favorite restaurants together and you can create your own private progressive dinner.

Those of us who live in cities often don't have enough time or money to sample all the restaurants in town. This is a perfect way to try out all those places. It would be ideal if most of the establishments were within walking distance of one another. Then you could walk off a few calories from the last course before you begin the next.

For Your Eyes Only

Women can never be told enough that they are loved and they are special. An inexpensive way of doing so is by sending a card or note. An inexpensive and clever way of doing so is by sending a *coded* card or note.

It is easy to come up with codes. You can use the standard 1=A, 2=B, 3=C, etc., or you can come up with a completely different code, using letters, numbers, or symbols of your own creation. If the code is simple enough, you may want to let her try to solve it on her own or for a complicated code, you might want to send the key to the code at a different time.

You can mail the coded message, fax it to her at work (her coworkers will be so envious), or place it in a book she is reading. You may want to cut out letters from magazines or newspapers to address the letter or fax so she won't recognize your handwriting. Watch out, 007!

Give a Gift They Are Guaranteed to Love

It really isn't that difficult to shop for women. Most of them love flowers, chocolate, and perfume. You really can't go wrong by buying one of those gifts for your wife or girlfriend. But is it what she *really* wants?

If you listen closely and pay good attention to what she is saying, you can discover what gift would make her overjoyed. However, don't expect her to drop hints on command. You must be listening for the clues at all times. She may indicate something she desires in May but you need to buy her something for her birthday in October.

Listen and watch for the clues and if necessary, write them down so when it becomes gift-buying time, you will know exactly what to purchase. Notice what she pampers herself with: tickets to the opera, coffee-table books, new CDs, trips to the spa, etc.

Have you ever noticed how she admires a piece of clothing or jewelry in a store's window display or on someone else? Does she look at magazines and show you an advertisement and say, "Wouldn't this look great in our dining room?" or "I would like to have something like this one day"? How about the time you went over to another couple's house and she really admired something there. A word of caution—just because she liked your neighbor's bread machine doesn't mean she would like one for an anniversary present. If you want to buy her a bread machine and surprise her with it one Sunday morning with a fresh loaf of bread baking in it, that would be fine. But don't give appliances or other impersonal gifts for special occasions!

lly, the next time she opens one of your gifts she
, "You shouldn't have!"—and really mean it.

Creative College Collage

Heather Tinkler
Tulsa, OK

My boyfriend and I have been dating for three years, and
for the last year and future one it's long distance because of
college. Right now we live two and a half hours apart, so
the weekends that I visit him are too few and far between.
So besides cards and surprise packages we try to include
"extras" while we're together.

Idea #1: Draw or cut out many fish pictures and paste
them on card stock. Hide them in places that you know
he/she will look but are still hidden, i.e., the refrigerator,
pockets, attached to the toothpaste tube, lamp switches,
etc., so that he or she will be "fishing" the whole day. Put
the last fish somewhere he or she will look last (on pillows,
under sheets) and write something like, "Of all the fishes
in the sea, I'm glad that you're the one for me."

Idea #2: I'm an art major, but my boyfriend is a botany/
chemistry major and a big part of our relationship is enjoying each other's interests. I researched his favorite plant (or-

it's the little things:
....

on a cold winter day put her towel in the dryer
while she is in the shower so it will be toasty
warm when she gets out

chids) and bought him one for his birthday. Not only did
he get a new plant but we were able to really talk about
something he is so passionate about. On his side, one of my
most prized possessions is a small drawing he did of the
two of us that I carry around in my wallet. It's extra special
since he's not at all artistic.

Idea #3: It's silly, but even though my boyfriend doesn't
wear cologne he always manages to smell terrific. Last time
I was down I swiped one of his slightly worn but not gross,
smelly T-shirts from the laundry (with permission of
course). When I got home I used it as a pillowcase. It's great
to have something to snuggle with when I miss him.

Idea #4: When in doubt, mix tapes! Our tastes in music
are extremely opposite but I made a tape for in the car of
alternate songs—one of his, one of mine, one of his, and so
on. This saves our sanity on road trips or even just going
to the store since there isn't any fighting over the radio station or a crazy mess of loose CDs and tapes.

Let It Snow, Let It Snow, Let It Snow

It was a rare snowy day in North Carolina. My wife was
working in a high rise downtown and I was going to pick
her up from work. At the time, she had an office on the

eighth floor which overlooked the street out front. Before she came down to the car, she would first look out her window just to make sure I was parked down below.

I took this unique opportunity to be a bit romantic. Before I left home, I took a squirt bottle and filled it with ice water and put a packet of cherry Kool-Aid in it. Any cold, red liquid would have worked just as well.

When I arrived in front of her office building, I quickly got out of the car and squirted I LOVE YOU on the white, snowy roof. It was important to use ice-cold water as even lukewarm water would have instantly melted the snow.

I knew Athena would look down and recognize the car and know instantly the message was meant for her, but I did not expect to see dozens of other faces peering out the office windows and calling their friends and coworkers over to look down at the curb below. In addition I got quite a few stares, smiles, and thumbs-up as people walked past me while I waited in the car for my wife to descend.

Even if your spouse doesn't work in a high rise with a window facing the street, you can adapt this idea to other occasions. You might have a two-story house with a lawn out front or back that can be a canvas for your creativity. In the fall you can create poetry with leaves and in the summer you can cut messages with a lawnmower. A slanted roof is another slate where you can leave your mark. Just be careful up there.

Icons of Love

There is no other time of the year more associated with romance than Valentine's Day. Its traditions and customs go far and deep. Just say the word *valentine* and images of rings and roses, hearts and cupids, flowers and fragrances instantly come to mind. The history behind these tokens of love comes from a time when a gift was more than a mere object, it was a way of communicating one's feelings instead of writing them on paper.

Don't simply buy a present because everyone else does. In your relationship, a red rose may have far less meaning than a wild orchid or a handful of daisies. A piece of jewelry might be somewhat trite compared to a wood carving you made just for her. A box of chocolates might scream "drugstore," while a better gift is a batch of her favorite pecan pralines you made yourself.

If you choose to celebrate Valentine's Day, don't do it out of a sense of obligation—do it as a celebration. Think hard about what customs and traditions are meaningful to your relationship. Don't simply mimic what millions of others are doing.

On Valentine's Day and at every other gift-giving occasion, make sure your presents come from the heart and not just from the wallet.

Kiss of the Week

There is a little game I play with my wife. I call it the kiss of the week. Each Sunday I designate a certain place to be the "kissing spot," and it is there that I softly plant my lips when I want to let her know I appreciate something she has done or to simply let her know that I love her.

I once heard an elderly man describe the success of his seventy-five-year blissful marriage to his wife. He attributed it to the fact that he told his wife daily that he loved her and kissed her at least twice each day. I aim to follow his example and by having the kissing spot of the week, it helps me to make certain I am not forgetting to give my wife the daily kisses she deserves so much.

Some of the kissing spots have been: behind her left ear,

between her eyes, the soft spot in the middle of her cheek, and on the nape of her neck. It's fun trying to decide where the next "spot" will be, and my wife looks forward to the new kiss at the beginning of the week. I do not forego kissing her on the lips, but I do make a conscious effort to kiss her often on the "kissing spot." If your wife hasn't been getting the kisses she deserves or you are looking for a way to be a more creative kisser, perhaps you too can implement the kiss of the week into your romantic lifestyle.

Bring the Rain Forest Indoors

Ah! A tropical rain forest! With its beautiful flowers, singing birds, and splashing waterfall you have an instant romantic adventure. No, I'm not about to tell you about a recent trip to some exotic country. Here is how you can have an enchanting rain forest in your own home.

It's so simple I am amazed I didn't think of it earlier. Fill your bathroom with as many plants as you can (no cactus, please). Bring in your music box and play your tape or CD of bird songs or tropical music (even certain types of Caribbean, Brazilian, or Hawaiian music would create the right atmosphere). With some duct tape and a dustpan you can easily transform your shower head into a waterfall (scrub the dustpan first).

If you want to go all out, replace your regular light bulbs with colored ones—blue and green would be a good choice to set the mood. Bring in some candles with tropical scents such as coconut, pineapple, and mango.

Now the next time your loved one needs a getaway but you don't have the time or the money, take their stress away with a tropical waterfall. It's a lot more creative than your average bubble bath with candles around the tub. Not only will your spouse thank you but your plants will enjoy the treatment as well.

A Gift to Remember

So you still don't know what to buy for that special occasion. Maybe it's your honey's fortieth birthday or your twenty-fifth anniversary. Here is a sure-fire hit.

It takes a few weeks or maybe even a few months of planning ahead, but the results will be no less than magical if you can pull it off. What I am speaking of is a *This Is Your Life* kind of gift. You will need to secretly obtain as many addresses and phone numbers of past and present friends, schoolmates, coworkers, and family. If your spouse is the kind of person who doesn't mind, sneaking through stashes of old letters and address books is one way to obtain the contacts. A better and perhaps less obtrusive way is to recruit a close friend or relative of the honoree to help you with your mission.

Either in a phone call or letter ask the people you contact if they would please contribute something memorable toward the upcoming special occasion. It could be old photographs, a story, something from a scrapbook, or just a note of congratulations. Also, ask them to pass the word along to anyone who may have known the person you will be honoring.

For secrecy you will need to have all the correspondence mailed to you at a location where it will not be seen by you-know-who. Have it mailed to your work address or maybe your coconspirator will agree to receive the mail. People are notorious about being procrastinators, so it will probably be necessary to remind them a week or two before the event to get the information to you, pronto.

Once you have received all the interesting tidbits, you will have to decide how to present them. You can present them in the world-famous *This Is Your Life* format with secret guests and a big production. What is more realistic would be providing a scrapbook filled with all the mementos and cards of congratulations. If you want something more dramatic like the *TIYL* format without all the work, you can read the letters and notes one by one, building up the suspense by not saying the contributor's name until the end. A nice photo album or scrapbook could be given so the honoree can put in all the pieces themselves.

If you know someone who is hard to shop for, this may just be the perfect gift for that momentous milestone in their life.

Why Married People Should Continue Dating

One of the biggest complaints from men and women about their spouses is how much they have changed since they were first dating.

We tend to put our best foot forward during the courting ritual, doing our utmost to impress our dates. We try to be polite, courteous, caring, giving, sensitive, well groomed, and well mannered. Then we get married (or engaged or move in together) and revert back to our old, self-centered, slovenly tendencies.

If you feel that your relationship may have lost some of its "spark," ask yourself if you are acting the same way as when you went out on those first few dates.

> ### it's the little things:
> ....
> a piece of chocolate placed on a pillow is the
> main ingredient in the recipe for sweet dreams

Can you imagine how different our relationships would be if we always behaved as though we were still wooing our significant other? We would belch, complain, argue, curse, whine, and nag much less. We would groom, smile, caress, encourage, give, clean, and communicate much more.

If you desire to keep that newlywed spark, you should never stop dating and courting the one you love, even after you exchange your vows.

Table for Two

For some people, the most romantic thing they do is take someone out to dinner. That is a kind gesture, especially if the person you are taking out does most of the cooking and washing up after meals.

I don't consider eating an ordinary meal at your average restaurant particularly romantic. Just because you take someone to a fancy or expensive restaurant, that doesn't make it romantic either. However, I do believe that dining at a restaurant (even your average chain variety) can be truly romantic with a little advanced preparation.

What makes dining out romantic are the elements of surprise, atmosphere, and thoughtfulness. Below are some suggestions on how to make your next dining experience *really* romantic.

♦ Bring flowers to the restaurant in advance and have the waiter deliver them after dessert.
♦ Arrange to have the musicians play "your song."
♦ Pretend to go to the restroom and give the waiter some jewelry or other present to be hidden in the dinner rolls.
♦ Go to the restaurant where you went on your first date (or proposed to her).
♦ Have the host slip a special note or card in the menu.
♦ Work with the chef in advance to prepare her favorite dishes (not all restaurants will do this).
♦ Create a fake menu that includes made-up dishes that have some sort of inside meaning or funny story.
♦ Arrange to have the waiter bring a small gift or card with every course.

Playing Your Cards Right

The other night Athena was sitting on the floor, folding a basket of clothes. I have never liked doing laundry or the dishes so I try to help out in other ways, like making dinner, picking up around the house, and taking care of the gardening. I don't think my wife likes to do the laundry either, but she does it every week and never complains about it. While I was watching her fluffing and folding shirts I began to think how thankful I was that my underwear drawer was never empty. I went into the bedroom and picked out a card from my secret stash and scribbled a quick note to thank her for always making sure my drawer was full of underwear and then placed it in the drawer for her to find when she was putting the freshly folded clothes away.

Because I had some blank greeting cards on hand, it was easy to do something nice on the spot while I was thinking about how much I appreciated my wife. I also keep a stack of cards at my office and regularly mail them to my wife's office or to her at home. Sometimes I will fill one out and put it in the car for her to find.

My wife particularly likes the Victorian cards that are reprints of cards used about a hundred years ago. I try to buy a variety and I concentrate on buying the ones that are blank inside so I can use them for nearly any occasion. The night my wife was doing laundry, I happened to have a card with a little girl washing something on a washboard. It looked as though I planned all week to have the card there when laundry day came up.

The Real Love Glove

Steve Casey
Shreveport, LA

During the years our children were growing up, we had our share of hospital visits. During the time spent with children at the hospital, I often used latex gloves to make balloon characters to decorate the children's rooms.

Recently, I found a way to use one of these latex gloves as a romantic gift. First, I turned the glove wrong side out. Then I tied the two middle fingers of the glove together, securing the knot but not pulling the base of the fingers too close together. Next, I turned the glove right side out and blew enough air into it to give it a good "hand" shape. This produced a hand with the little finger, index finger, and thumb out, forming the well-known sign language symbol for "I love you." I then tied off the glove.

With a felt-tip pen I wrote an I and a U on the palm of the hand and placed a heart sticker in between the letters. After placing a few more heart stickers on the glove, I used double-sided sticky padding to secure the bottom of the glove to a small ceramic toothpick holder so that it would stand up appropriately. When my wife came home from her job at the hospital, I had my "love glove" where she would soon find it.

Breakfast of Champions

It was a tradition in our house that on Mother's Day the family would prepare breakfast and bring it to Mom in bed. Unfortunately for Mom, Mother's Day came along only once a year. I don't see how anyone who cleans the house, makes the meals, does the laundry, and runs the errands 365 days a year can be justly rewarded by only one day of breakfast in bed.

I have heard of cases where a husband has made it a ritual to make breakfast or brunch every Saturday or Sunday for the family to give his wife at least one day a week to sleep late. Is it too much to ask to bring your wife breakfast in bed once a month? You don't even have to know how to cook to do it. Here are some ideas of simple menu items you could put together for a much appreciated breakfast in bed. If you are able to create a more elaborate meal, all the better.

If you bring her a breakfast that you have created, no matter how simple, you will be a champion in her eyes.

◆ Cereal with fresh fruit
◆ Toast or English muffin with butter and jam
◆ Half an orange or grapefruit
◆ Bagel with cream cheese
◆ Yogurt with fresh fruit
◆ Coffee/tea in a nice cup
◆ Orange juice served in a crystal glass
◆ A chocolate truffle

To make this breakfast look more elaborate, include a flower in a vase, a cloth napkin, and decorate the plate with a sprig of herb or a thin slice of fruit. You can put a hand-written card or note on the tray for added impact.

MEMO

TO: *My Darling*

FROM: *Your Best Friend*

How to Have an Office Romance

When Athena was working outside of the home, we would meet at her office to go have lunch together. One particular day she was away from her desk when I arrived and I had a feeling she wouldn't be back for five or ten minutes.

I spied a small packet of yellow sticky notes on her desk and went to work. I wrote about a dozen short messages and quickly hid them all throughout her cubicle. On one, I wrote "I love you" and I stuck it in her Rolodex under the letter L.

I hid one under her water bottle, inside the phone cradle, in her candy dish, and several more in out-of-the-way locations. I even hid a note in the paper station of her printer so when it was time to replace the paper she would find it there. On her message pad I went down a few pages and wrote a message.

TO: Athena
FROM: Your Best Friend
MESSAGE: Missing you—come home soon.

Several days each week she would let me know she had discovered one of her notes. She found most of them before she quit her job. I think there were still a couple for her replacement to find. Hope they make her day.

Is Your Relationship in Neutral?

Many men have the impression that as long as they are not yelling at their wives, beating them, cheating on them, or leaving huge messes around the house, they must be good husbands. All that means is that they aren't bad husbands. They are probably just average husbands. Instead of not just yelling at their wives, husbands should make an effort to say lots of wonderful things to their wives. Instead of not just beating his wife, a husband should make certain he often lovingly touches her: stroking her hair, lightly kissing her neck, gently massaging her shoulders, kindly rubbing her feet, and giving her light kisses on her cheek, nose, ears, forehead, and of course, lips. A man shouldn't only not cheat on his wife, he should passionately seduce her. Not being a total slob isn't bad, but helping your wife with the chores is even better. Giving her a whole day or week off from her usual chores and you doing them for her is best.

Men should never settle for being average. If your relationship has been in neutral, it's time for you to move into first gear.

Preventing the Out-of-Town-Business Blues

One of my wife's friends was boasting the other day that her husband had been out of town for a week and a half and he had already called twice! He called her on two different occasions during the ten days he had been away. In other words, he called every five days. Imagine how excited she would have been if he had called every day or every other day!

How much pocket change and how many minutes does it take to make a phone call each day to let the one you love know that you are thinking of them while you are out of town? And how much does it cost to send a card? If you can call in to the office every day to check in or see if you have any messages, shouldn't you be able to call home every night?

Besides making phone calls, another way to let your mate know that you are thinking of them while away on business is to bring home some gifts. You don't need to spend a lot of money. In fact, you don't have to spend any money. Bring home a toiletry item from the hotel, a matchbook from a restaurant, a brochure about the city you visited, or other souvenirs from the trip. Then when your wife asks you to tell her about the trip (and she certainly will), you can give her the items, explaining where you went and what you did. The fact that you took the time to collect these seemingly insignificant items will mean more to her than you could imagine because she'll know you were thinking of her each day.

Also, if you know in advance that you will be going away on a business trip without your wife or girlfriend, you can plan on having greeting cards arrive home several of the days you are gone. You will need to gauge ahead of time how long it takes for mail to arrive to your house from different locations and plan accordingly. You may want to mail some from near your home, some from work, and perhaps some from your business trip. Typically, a letter can go anywhere in the states within four days, and post-cards take a couple of days longer. Even if a letter or card arrives after you have returned, your wife/girlfriend will still be suitably impressed and will certainly be boasting to her friends how you are such a fabulous husband/boyfriend.

it's the little things:

preparing your spouse's toothbrush is another way
of kissing them good morning and good night

Waking Up Is Hard to Do

My wife wakes up about twenty minutes before I do. She
takes a shower and then comes back to bed and wakes me
up by giving me "wake-up kisses." She kisses both my eye-
lids, then my nose, then the two corners of my mouth, my
forehead, both my ears, and then my chin.

Morning is not my favorite time of day and I don't relish
having to get out of bed early in the morn. However, those
waking kisses make the transition from sleeping to waking
much easier, and enjoyable.

Does your spouse have trouble getting up in the morning? Help her start the day off right with a few wake-up
kisses. I do recommend brushing your teeth and using
mouthwash first so the kisses are fresh and clean. Of course
the smell of stale breath might wake her too, but you want
her first waking moment to be one of pleasure, not pain.

Send Your Love Electronically

With the increasing popularity of the Internet and other
computer message boards, more people than ever are
tapped into the computer. It doesn't have to be a cold medium. A little loving message found on the home computer
can warm up anyone's day. Most of us spend a great deal
of time on the computer every week. Why not take a small

amount of that time to send a message to the person who means the most to you?

Most people enjoy getting mail. I certainly do. I look forward to hearing "you've got mail" from my computer whenever I log online. Some computer mail systems can be programmed to send messages at specific times or on an exact day in the future. If your wife gets on the computer often, you can program dozens of messages at once to be sent all throughout the month. By programming your computer to send either a message to yourself or your wife, it is a great way to be certain that you don't forget a birthday or anniversary. To make that special occasion even more special you could arrange for your spouse to receive dozens (if not hundreds) of computer messages from friends, family, and even complete strangers. There are many chat rooms or bulletin boards where you could make your wishes be known. Depending on where you post your request, congratulatory messages might come in from all over the world.

While dozens of personalized messages received will definitely lift anyone's day, even one small message sent to your wife's e-mail address will bring a guaranteed smile to her face. Make sure the messages are sent to her home e-mail, unless she works at a company that allows personal e-mail to be sent there.

The World's Best Bandage

My wife banged her head the other day. It made a nice-size bump on her forehead. As soon as it happened I went over and gently kissed it. And she instantly felt better.

I always kiss her "ouches" even if she doesn't ask me to. I know there is nothing magical in my kisses. Why do children want their bumps and scrapes kissed? They associate kisses with love and healing in a time when they are aching. A kiss is simply a physical way of showing someone that you recognize their pain, that you are concerned about it, and that you will do whatever it takes to make them feel better.

The next time your wife gets hurt, kiss it and you will make it all better.

Romance on a Budget

Looking to celebrate a holiday or a special occasion? Being a downscaler can pay off big. In romance, ingenuity counts more than cash. Consider these ideas from Edith Kilgo, editor of *Creative Downscaling* newsletter.

Go for nostalgia: Give your beloved a gift recalling the tender days of your courtship: a photo collage; a book of poetry you read together long ago; an enlarged and framed favorite snapshot.

Give a serenade: Tapes of romantic music you've enjoyed in the past are good, but even better is a music box that plays "your song."

Plant one: Roses are expensive. Consider a tree instead. What? You don't think a tree is romantic? Ever hear of moonlight and magnolias?

Candy is dandy: Forget the standard chocolates. Most of us have some kind of nostalgic yearning for something mundane that's hard to find. Whether it's gum drops or jelly beans, go to the extra trouble to find what he or she really craves. A good place to find old-fashioned candy is in the Vermont Country Store catalog (802-362-2400).

Make a special evening: Maybe you can't afford much, but a home-cooked meal, a luxurious bubble bath, and a massage are always welcome.

Serve up a theme: Serve him a heart-shaped cake. Give her a locket. Rent a romantic film at the video store. Take a heart-healthy, long, moonlight walk together.

Get framed: Poetry is nice, but most of us aren't up to it. Instead, write your beloved a letter of praise. Have it copied in calligraphy script and framed.

Create a romance basket: Choose any or all of the following to present in a pretty basket: romantic music on cassette or CD; a favorite video or a wonderful love story; a classic love story in paperback; love poems; bath crystals; your favorite drink; two scented candles; and a wonderful edible in just two servings.

Take over a chore: Does your sweetie hate washing the car or making dinner? Even if you aren't good at it, the effort will be appreciated.

Revisit your childhood: Make a crepe-paper box and stuff it with declarations of your love. It's better than a store-bought card.

Fun with Flowers

Terri Powers
Denver, CO

I loved your story about gift wrap ideas [see It's a Wrap on page 75] and just thought I would share one more with you. I was wrapping a wedding present and realized I had no bows or ribbon. Instead of going to the store to buy some I hit upon the idea of using potpourri.

The mix I had included dried rosebuds, leaves, and other flowers. I used a hot-glue gun to create a centerpiece "arrangement" on the paper. Not only did it look great but it smelled wonderful too!

It also occurred to me that the recipient could save the paper with the potpourri intact and put it in a frame with raised glass as a decorative item. If a spouse were to wrap a special gift like this, they could secretly save the paper after it's opened to present a framed memento later on.

Star Light, Star Bright

A few months ago I was going to be out of town for a few days and wanted to do something that would help Athena remember me while I was away. I came up with the idea of sleeping under the stars.

No, we did not sleep outside. Instead, I brought the stars inside. I went to a toy store and bought a package of glow-in-the-dark star stickers. There were several dozen if not a hundred or so stars in the package. When my wife was out running some errands, I stood on our bed and arranged the stars on our bedroom ceiling. This would work by putting them on a mobile too.

That night I turned on all the lights in the bedroom for an hour or so before we were going to sleep. The glow-in-the-dark chemicals in the stars need light to energize.

When we finally lay down to go to sleep, I turned off the light and my wife looked up to see the whole ceiling aglow. She was amazed at the spectacle. I told her that whenever she looks at the ceiling at night she should think of me. I came back from my trip and the stars are still up. I think I will keep them up there a little while longer. It's fun sleeping under the stars.

Love Is Only a Page Away

Most likely, a large percentage of the readers of this book carry a pager. I carried one for several years. It certainly can be a nuisance at times. However, it can also be one more way to let someone know you are thinking of them.

Recently, alpha-numeric pagers have been becoming increasingly popular. You can simply type in a message and the pager will automatically display it. On the other hand, numbers-only pagers require a little more creativity in sending over "love messages."

As you probably know, numbers look like certain letters when held upside down. One of the more well-known of such words is 07734 (hello).

You can also type in 143, 1 for letter I, 4 to signify the number of letters in *love*, and 3 for the letters in *you*.

Here are a few others for you to try out on your sweetheart:

```
5376616(giggles)
53551,5604(hogs & isses)-hugs & kisses
372215(sizzle)
55178(bliss)
14(hi)
5637(legs)
55378(bless)
```

Bathtub Bliss

Does your wife or girlfriend ever have a rough day? Of course she does. Sometimes, those days are even predictable. My wife is often exhausted on Fridays because of all the last-minute projects at work that have to be finished before the weekend. Students and teachers are often fatigued at the end of exams. Mothers are tired at the end of every day.

Here's an idea that is bound to take the stress away. If you know your wife is going to be in need of some special pampering, you can sneak into the bathroom and arrange a hot bubble bath for her. If the circumstances do not warrant you being able to do that, you can simply put all the necessary items in a nice basket or box and give it as a gift. (For a really clever way of presenting this gift, see Bathtub Bubbles on page 72.)

Here are some items that you should consider putting in the bathroom or in your gift basket:

- Bubble bath
- Soothing tape or CD
- Candles
- Bath oils or herbs
- Snacks (chocolates are always a winner)
- A bath pillow
- Natural sponge
- Book of poetry
- Large glass of lemonade, ice water, wine, or liqueur
- Comfortable robe for after the bath

Puzzle Your Spouse

If you are searching for a gift or simply want an activity that you and your significant other can do together, consider puzzling. I am the first to admit that just sitting down and talking can get boring rapidly. One way to keep conversations alive while not going out of your mind is to bond over a puzzle. Not only will the time spent together talking be of importance, the sense of team accomplishment when the puzzle is complete can be rewarding too. Many people enjoy puzzling because it usually relieves stress. However, I did have one puzzle—a night sky—that was nearly all black, which caused a lot of stress.

If you would like to put a romantic twist on this idea, you can go to a craft or toy store and buy a blank puzzle. You can draw your own message or picture on the puzzle and then take it apart before presenting it to your wife.

Another source for puzzles are photo-developing companies that will turn photographs into puzzles.

If You Love Them, Book Them

NBC News labeled me the "World's Most Romantic Man." I don't really think I deserve the title but it's fun to have anyway. It would be a great pickup line, but fortunately I am very happily married to a wonderful, beautiful, bright, caring, gentle, kind woman and have no need of pickup lines.

One of the reasons many people in the media have said that I am so romantic is that I like to celebrate my wedding anniversary every month (see That Time of the Month on page 4). In celebration of my seventy-fifth (monthly) anniversary with my wife, I decided to create a gift that would help us reflect back on our first six and a quarter years of marriage.

I came up with the idea of creating a coloring book for my wife. I took a sheet of paper and tried to write down the most significant, memorable, and happy experiences we had since we were married. I even took out our scrapbooks to make sure I wasn't missing any major events. Once I had about thirty ideas I began sketching them on plain white paper. I admit I am not much of an artist but even stick figures can get an idea across.

Once I completed doodling all the scenes with pencil, I traced over them with a black felt-tip pen, and wrote what the occasion was just in case my drawing was so bad that she wouldn't be able to decipher the event. I emphasized the childlike look of the book by writing with my left hand.

Once all the sketches were complete I drew a cover and then took them to a copy store and had all the pages duplicated onto heavy paper and then bound. I even made an extra in case she wanted one without coloring in it.

Give it with a pack of crayons and you're in business.

Computer Romance

Here are a few more ideas on using the computer to be a romantic. I won't try to instruct you in the technical ways in which to do these ideas, as I would probably add more confusion than direction.

◆ Change the screen saver to a marquee that has a loving message.
◆ If you have a microphone, you may be able to change or add greetings that will sound whenever your wife logs on or off the computer or does some other function.

- Create a love letter on the computer and send your wife on a computer scavenger hunt to try to find it.
- Scan a photograph of you and your wife to be used as the wallpaper on your computer.
- Create notes all throughout your system and name them with file names such as "iloveyou" or "lookhere" so they will catch her eye and she will open them.
- While you're at it, visit *The RoMANtic* on the Internet at http://www.TheRomantic.com for more ideas.

Our Most Romantic Piece of Furniture

There is a very romantic piece of furniture in our house. You probably can't guess what it is.

The trend of these last couple of decades is to divide everything into "his" and "hers." There are his and hers towels. His and hers sinks. His and hers recliners. His and hers checking accounts. The more things are divided means there are less things to be shared.

When Athena and I bought our first house in North Carolina my mother wanted to buy us a special house-warming present. We asked her to pitch in on a chair and a half. That's right. Not one chair to fight over or two chairs to separate us. We wanted to have one chair that we could share *together*.

A chair and a half is an extra-wide chair that can fit two average-size persons. It is also extra long so it is like having a built-in ottoman. Some people call it a two-person chaise.

When we watch a movie we do so side by side, not separated. Even watching the news can be a romantic occasion for us as I wrap my arms around Athena while we view the weekend weather update. During our midday tea break we will often have our "cuppa" in *our* chair.

Too much "personal space" can kill a relationship. I think we all need more "shared space."

Counting Down to a Happy Holiday

There is a traditional eastern European Christmas gift called an advent calendar. It is typically a box with "doors" covering each day counting down to Christmas Day. Behind each door is a small treat, usually a chocolate or a type of toy found in a Cracker Jacks box. Most of the ones sold in specialty stores in the United States have a different candy behind each door.

You could certainly use this idea for Christmas and replace the candies and toys with other gifts such as jewelry, poetry, concert/movie tickets, chocolates, perfumes, or other items that would bring her joy. However, this idea is not limited to the winter holidays. It is one that could be used all throughout the year. You could count down a week or a month before any special occasion—like an anniversary or birthday. Either you can buy an advent calendar and replace the insides with something a bit more from the heart or you could make one completely from scratch.

You don't even have to use the typical advent calendar. You could buy small boxes from a stationery or card store and write the date on the outside of each box when it is to be opened. Or you could do the same with plastic Easter eggs and put them in a basket to be cracked open one day at a time.

I like the idea of putting in clues to be discovered each day which will hint to the gift that will be given on the anniversary or birthday. Be certain to make the first clues difficult, because if she figures it out right away, it will spoil the fun for the both of you.

As you can see, you can have a lot of fun with this idea. There are dozens of ways it can be altered to creatively count down to something special.

Plan the Perfect Picnic

Spring is the perfect time for a picnic. Trees are flowering, birds are singing, and the weather is so delightful. So why would anyone want to spend spring in a movie theater? It is no secret that going to the movies is probably the most popular form of entertainment. I enjoy a good movie myself, but when the weather is beautiful, I prefer to be entertained by the outdoors.

When was the last time you went on a picnic? When

was the last time you went on a *secret* picnic? You can plan a picnic and tell your spouse all about it or, to make it more romantic, you can keep the plans under wraps.

There are several ways you can pull off the surprise. You can suggest going to a movie or out to lunch, but end up driving to the countryside or to your favorite city park to have a picnic. Once I planned a secret picnic with the help of my friends. I gave my girlfriend (who is now my wife) directions to where we were going. However, I wrote them in the form of riddles. I used street names and landmarks in the clues and eventually we made it across town to a park where a picnic (prepared by me but put there by my friends) was waiting for us. Another way of pulling off the surprise is to go to the park and have the food delivered to you. You could order pizza, or many restaurants now offer delivery service. You would still have to provide your own blanket and utensils.

Secret picnics are very easy to pull off because you don't have to plan far ahead and you can hide everything in the trunk of your car. Here is a list of possible items you can include in your picnic:

♦ Strawberries, grapes, or other fresh fruit
♦ Cheese and crackers
♦ Bagels and cream cheese
♦ Pickles, olives, and baby corn
♦ Chocolates
♦ Cookies, cake, or other dessert
♦ Champagne or sparkling juice
♦ Kite, if it is a windy day
♦ Radio or CD player
♦ Book of poetry to read out loud

If you don't have the time to gather the food together, many gourmet grocery stores provide ready-made baskets or will put one together for you.

Don't forget really important items like cups, plates, napkins, utensils, can openers, cutting knives, and a blanket and small pillow for her.

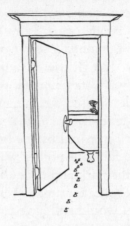

Kiss the Ground

Phil Dunbridge
Claremont, CA

It feels so good to know that there are others like myself: not naturally romantic, but really taking the whole idea to the extreme. I would like to tell you a story of something I did for my girlfriend. It was my senior year (her junior year) in high school and I wanted to ask her to the prom in a really nice way. So I got a house key from her mother, and went in one day while she was at work. I made a trail of Hershey's kisses from her front door, all the way up to her bathroom. I then put a dozen roses in her bathtub. Then I continued the trail into her bedroom. On her bed I placed a single rose, and a card that read: "Now that I have kissed the ground you walk on, and showered you with roses, will you go to the prom with me?"

Her response was many tears of happiness. This can work for many other things besides asking your loved one to a dance.

Please keep up the good work. I feel that the majority of women today have come to the conclusion that people like you and I do not exist, so they allow men to walk all over them. No one deserves that.

Rain, Rain, Don't Go Away

Rain can be very depressing. It can also be extremely refreshing. If rain puts you in the doldrums, consider trying out a few of the ideas below to turn stormy weather into a unique and romantic experience:

- Take a walk together without an umbrella and stomp in the puddles.
- Make a cup of hot tea, hot chocolate, or coffee and drink it with biscotti or some other cookies.
- Play Scrabble or some other board game.
- Turn out all the lights, light candles, and listen to some jazz or soft music.
- Light a fire and sip brandy or your favorite liqueur.
- Bake cookies with your spouse.

When a Kiss Is Not Just a Kiss

When my wife and I were dating in college, I began using a Hershey's kiss as my signature. I would hide them in ice-cream cones. I would have her roommates place them on her pillow. I would have waiters bring them with the check. I would even mail them to her. I wanted her to think of me at all times of the day. Giving her these "kisses" was very inexpensive and didn't take much time at all. However, they spoke volumes of my love for her.

There are many different signatures you can use to quietly say you love her. At many stationery stores I have seen sheets of tiny red hearts (and smiley faces). They could be stuck on notes, windshields, lunch bags, calendars, toothpaste tubes, alarm clocks, and endless other places. The idea is not to blanket everything at once with your signature but to leave them every so often and perhaps for the rest of your life. I still leave "kisses" for my wife to discover.

Another idea for a signature is a comic strip of her liking. You would either need to be diligently cutting it out of the paper or buy a book from which to cut it out. Some Christian bookstores sell stacks of small cards with inspirational scriptures on them that could be used as your signature as well.

At first you might want to begin by sending a card or small present or two with your new signature on them so she will get the idea when she starts seeing it pop up all over the place.

What is going to be your signature?

The Bear Essentials

Are you ever away from your spouse for several days because of business or other reasons? I think that is a perfect time to let her know just how much you care for her and how attentive you are to her needs.

An ideal way of reminding your wife of you while you are away is through a stuffed animal. Teddy bears and all of their stuffed cousins make perfect surrogate mates. They can do almost everything on your behalf while you are gone. They will listen endlessly to your wife and not complain once. They will share dinner with her and eat with impeccable manners. They will even cuddle with her all night long without expecting anything in return.

This idea will also work if your wife is the one who will be away from home for several days. Mr. Bear makes a perfect traveling companion. You can send him along with her or even have him waiting at her destination.

I would recommend writing a note and attaching it to the stuffed animal explaining why you are giving it to her. Without a note, it is simply a nice gift. With a note of explanation, it becomes a meaningful thought that will occupy her mind for many, many days.

To extend the idea even further, you can send a letter to Mr. Bear or whatever stuffed animal you sent. Send it in care of your wife. Of course she will be the one who reads it, but in the letter you can state things like, "You know I love my wife very, very much and I want you to protect her while I am away. Also, make sure she gets plenty of rest and eats her vegetables while I am gone. If it thunders at night, put your arm around her to keep her from being afraid." I know it sounds a bit silly, but believe me, it will make a big impression.

In addition to notes and letters, you can have the bear give presents to your wife on your behalf. You can put a necklace around the bear's neck, and some stuffed animals even come with backpacks that could be filled with all sorts of gifts.

If you or your loved one is frequently out of town, this is one idea that can be used over and over. Just attach a new letter, card, or present and you are set.

Showering Her with Love

George Garcia
San Luis Obispo, CA

This past spring, I decided to throw a shower and brunch for my wife, who was expecting our second child. Planning a shower in and of itself is unremarkable; however, having a shower planned by the husband is unheard of, at least in our circle of friends. My wife's girlfriends said it was a "very sweet" thing to do, secretly thinking I was never going to pull it off.

Armed with a stack of my wife's back issues of *Martha Stewart Living*, I planned the menu, negotiated a venue, assembled a guest list, and hired a harpist. If I had known how much work this little shower was going to be, I would have taken the easier way out and bought my wife a minivan.

With the help of some very understanding friends, I began cooking at 6:00 P.M. the day before the brunch. Seventeen hours later, the guests began to arrive. Appetizers, which consisted of twice-baked new potatoes stuffed with caviar, baked palmiers filled with prosciutto, Dijon mustard, and Romano cheese, and a local California champagne were all served to the sounds of a live harpist. Salmon crepes with crème fraîche accompanied by rosemary-garlic red potatoes were served as the main entrée. White buttercream cake topped with candied pansies finished the day. I have to admit that because my wife found out about the shower beforehand (it was supposed to be a surprise), and because she is by far the better baker, I asked her to prepare the cake. It was wonderful. The entire event went off without a hitch.

The Unprom

Alan Staney
Tallahassee, FL

My last girlfriend was definitely *not* your average girl. She absolutely hated getting flowers, getting dressed up, going out to dinner, all the usual dating stuff. But I, on the other hand, was a deeply romantic person. And I tried very hard to parallel those kind of things in our relationship.

The prom was around the corner, a time both of us had dreaded the whole year. Being seventeen, we were virtually required to go. So, I invited her *not* to go to the prom with me, which sounded a little strange, but I was determined to do something that night knowing that everyone else would wake up the next morning with memories of a very magical night, which I would be jealous of.

I didn't like getting dressed up, but that didn't mean I had to miss out.

So I invented a way to parallel everyone else's night out with my own event, a "fake prom," one that I thought my girlfriend would enjoy. She had told me way beforehand that she hated getting flowers and all of that, but I remembered that she always had a ChupaChups lollipop in her hand. So I bought a dozen ChupaChups which I presented to her like a bouquet. Then we went to pick up dinner . . . at a Subway (sandwich restaurant). If it was anything more romantic, she would have killed me, which makes me wonder how we ended up together. . . .

The week before, I had made a tape of all kinds of love songs. Equipped with music, I took her downtown, where I knew how to get on the rooftops using a statue.

We had our dinner during the sunset up above the city, then danced the night away under the stars, above the streetlights. We later went to the park and swung for a while, played on the playground (being seventeen is wonderful . . .), and then I took her home at 11:00 sharp—I was never late on curfew. We had a wonderful night, one that I'll never forget.

A Loving Lunch

I know this specific idea won't apply to most men, but hopefully you can take the idea and alter it to an occasion that is practical for you. Also, I know that many women will buy this book and use its ideas because, as they often write to me saying, "I know my husband will never be a romantic, but that shouldn't stop me from being one" and "We need creative ideas too!"

Specifically, this essay is about packing a lunch for your love. I used to pack my wife's lunch when she worked in an office and I worked at home. I tried to help her out in the mornings as she was rushing off to work.

Here are a few ways in which I tried to "spice" up her lunch now and again to let her know just how much I care:

- Carve a message on an apple or pear in the morning and by lunchtime, the message will "magically" appear.
- Draw cartoons or write notes on a napkin.
- Include Hershey's kisses or other wrapped chocolates. Write a short note on the inside of the wrapper.
- Put in a favorite comic strip.
- Write a short story and send it in installments.
- On sandwiches draw a heart on the bread with mustard or ketchup from a squirt bottle. You need to leave something off the sandwich like tomatoes or lettuce for them to add later so they will see it.

↓

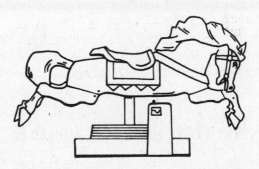

Hey Man, Can You Spare a Quarter?

I've got a pocketful of quarters and what shall I do? Go on a date!

Do you have a change jar with a lot of quarters? Time for a "quarter date." The quarter date can be quite adventurous—it all depends on how you spend your change. The parameter of this date is to spend approximately ten dollars' worth of quarters in machines.

It sounds a little difficult at first thought, but once your mind starts racing, you will be able to come up with a whole slew of ideas. Here are some places quarters are gladly accepted:

♦ The kiddie rides in front of Wal-Mart and other stores (good place to get a soft drink, as they often cost only twenty-five cents there).
♦ Of course you can go to an arcade, but don't blow all of your coins there. Only play games the two of you can enjoy together, like air hockey or pinball.
♦ Go somewhere where there are those tourist binoculars on stands.
♦ Stroll through a toy store and play with the toys, then upon leaving get something out of the gumball or prize machines.
♦ Go to a photo booth (located in some malls and drugstores) and have some fun shots taken.
♦ You can toss your quarters in wishing wells and fountains or tip a strolling street musician. I know they aren't machines, but they sure are romantic.

When Love Has a Nice Ring to It

Since the days of early Rome, the ring has been a symbol of love. Its unbroken shape represents eternity and since that time has been used as a lover's pledge.

Egyptian physicians thought that the nerves on the left "ring" finger and right middle finger led straight to the heart. Hence the tradition was born as to where to wear a wedding ring.

In addition, gems began to symbolize certain aspects of relationships. Over time, the diamond became the chief stone for engagements, probably due to its brilliance and clarity, which symbolized purity, and its strength, which represented an enduring love. While the "unspoken" meaning for most stones has died in the past century, it doesn't mean they can't be resurrected for the right occasion.

If you are buying a ring for your love, here is one way of presenting it to her creatively. First, bake her a small cake. Of course it should be one of her favorites. When the cake has baked and cooled, tie one end of a small ribbon around the ring and gently insert the ring into the cake. Then frost and decorate the cake. Either make the remainder of the ribbon part of the decoration or tie it in a bow and rest it on top of the cake. When you are serving this dessert, you simply have your sweetheart pull the ribbon to reveal her present.

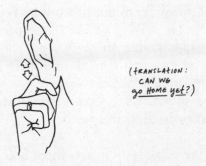

(tRANSLAtioN:
CAN WG
go HoME yet?)

The Silent Language

I often wish Athena and I knew sign language. That way I could easily tell her how beautiful she is from across a crowded room.

Not knowing sign language does not keep me from communicating with her when we are no longer within earshot of each other. I've been known to make all sorts of gestures from across the room with my hands, eyes, and lips. I guess you would call that flirting.

I know some people actually come up with certain hand signals to say "I love you" silently. I have heard of those that will do so by touching their finger to the tip of their nose. Some will raise one finger, followed by four, and then three—signifying the number of letters in that special phrase. Of course you can point to your eye, then your heart, and then your sweetheart to get the message across.

Once you have mastered the "I love you" you can move on to more difficult phrases by tugging on your ear, tapping your chin, rubbing your temple, and other signals. If pitchers and coaches can do it, why can't lovers?

Return to Sender

Have you ever received flowers from someone? Most of us have. Do you throw them out when they begin to wilt? Most of us do.

Why not consider saving those flowers and returning them to the one who sent them? Sound rude or strange? Actually, it can be quite romantic.

There are a few different ways you can prepare the flowers for their journey back to their giver.

♦ Take some of the flowers and press them between sheets of wax paper in the pages of a dictionary or other large book. It will take several weeks or months for the flowers to properly flatten and dry, but the results will be worth it. Then you may want to frame the blossoms behind glass, create a card and glue them on the front, or iron them between two pieces of laminating paper to be preserved forever.

♦ The second way to preserve flowers is to remove the blossoms from their stems and dry them to make potpourri. There are several ways to dry whole flowers or just the petals. You can do it with an oven, microwave, silica crystals (found in craft stores), or simply air-dry them. You may want to check out a book from the library that would give instructions on drying flowers and perhaps a book that would give some recipes on making potpourri. You can put in whole spices like cinnamon and cloves or dried orange peels for additional fragrance. Many craft stores sell oils that can be added to dried petals for an array of smells.

♦ A third way of preparing flowers for a return shipment is to make a dried flower arrangement. Again, you may want to consult a book on how to dry flowers. I have had good success with drying whole flowers by hanging them upside down in a dark, dry closet for a couple of weeks. It is important to begin the process before the petals begin to fall off the flowers. Once the flowers are dry, arrange them (or have someone help you if you have no talent in this area) and put them in a vase. You can buy an ordinary vase or search flea markets or antique stores for an old teapot or brass pot to go with your arrangement.

♦ The fourth way you can return the flowers to their sender is to save all the petals and return them in a crystal bowl or vase. A friend of mine dried the petals from all the roses her boyfriend had given her and they looked strikingly beautiful in a crystal vase.

These gifts are not the same as buying potpourri or a dried flower arrangement from the store down the road. These are gifts that have history and meaning. You received these flowers, adored and cherished them and then took the initiative to preserve them, for everlasting enjoyment.

Imagine the reaction you would get if on the night you asked your girlfriend to become your wife, you presented her with the first flower she had given to you two or three years earlier.

If fresh flowers can enable one to feel the warmth of someone's love, imagine what returned flowers can do.

Make a Rose

Have you ever given someone a rose? Has anyone ever given you a rose? On your wedding day did your bride have roses in her bouquet?

This is an idea that will take a lot of patience, a bit of luck, and perhaps a little assistance from some friends or family.

Let's just take as an example a bride who has roses in her bouquet. If you are crafty enough, you can retrieve some of the roses from the person who catches the bouquet (I don't know any woman who wouldn't go along with this after you explained what you are doing).

Now the more difficult part. You need to cut off the head of the rose and a small amount from the bottom of the stem. You need to dip the bottom in a rooting hormone (easily obtained from any nursery), then plant it in a container of half Perlite and half soil. Keep the soil moist until the stems have rooted. If this sounds like it is way out of your league, then ask a friend or family member with a green thumb to give you a little assistance. You might even find a compassionate woman at a nursery who would do this for you for little or no charge.

Then on your first anniversary or other special occasion you can give a present of rose bushes that will have more meaning than all the dozen roses you could ever give.

Prescription for Happiness

Paul J. Hartstirn
Columbus, IN

Some pharmacies are very agreeable to make up prescription labels with whatever you want printed on them (for free!). The label and little "pill" container I had made up had these elements:

DR.: Feelbetter
PATIENT: Amy Hartstirn
INSTRUCTIONS: Blow three (3) seconds by mouth for fighting children and repeat as needed.
CONTENTS: Referee's whistle

I gave it to my wife to help stop fights between the kids. The pharmacy put the whistle in a pill container, and sealed it all up in a pharmacy bag. It looked like a real prescription! She loved it.

There are many different variations to this theme which could be used for special surprises: anniversary rings, new car keys, ear plugs to block out the kids' noise, a coupon for a night out, a small bottle of perfume, etc. The labels can be put on boxes . . . so you're not restricted to pill-bottle-size items.

Begin Thinking Like a Romantic

In the hundreds of interviews I have given, one question continually comes up. The reporters want to know where I get my ideas. The answer is quite simple: everywhere!

Very few men are natural romantics. All of us have the capability of being romantic, it just takes a little effort and practice. After years of practice, the way my mind processes information has changed. When I read the newspaper, walk through a store, or watch a movie, my mind latches on to ideas that could be used to express my love to my wife. As I mentioned in a previous idea, even the junk mail can be a source for romantic inspiration.

Several new ideas come to me each day. In fact, I have so many ideas that I will not be able to use all of them in my lifetime. I challenge you to write down one romantic idea each day for the next week. You will discover that it is a lot easier than it seems. You may even be able to write down several each day. Once you train your mind to think as a romantic, the ideas will begin appearing without any effort at all.

Go Fly a Kite – Seriously

I can't think of a much more romantic Sunday afternoon than a picnic followed by kite flying on a blustery day. One of the most romantic aspects of kite flying can be the making of the kites.

Kites are relatively simple to make. All you need are some wooden rods, string, small nails, glue, and some sort of paper such as wax paper or parchment paper. I think it is fun to work on designing and building the kites together or have a competition to see who can make the kite that will fly the highest. If you want to go all out, you can also make a fancy tail for a kite using pieces of scrap material you may have lying around the house.

If you check out a book on kite making at the library, you can see how to make box kites, acrobatic kites, or other unique kite creations. Just remember that the most important aspect of kite making and kite flying is the time spent together.

Gather your materials, make a few sandwiches, turn on the radio, and have a wonderful time making your kites together. Then go find an open, windy place to test out your creation.

The Importance of Romantic Rituals

My wife, Athena, and I have a daily ritual which I think strengthens our marriage. When she comes home from work each day (my office is in the house), we catch up with each other over a pot of hot tea. We learned to appreciate the daily ritual of taking tea after a visit to England.

With tea we usually have a couple of cookies, banana bread, or some other small snack item. While polishing off the pot of tea we sit for thirty minutes or so and discuss how the day went and what our plans might be for that night or the rest of the week. We also discuss future plans and dreams or whatever is on our minds. It is a very worthwhile ritual and one that we plan on continuing indefinitely.

Many couples with children often ask me how they can add romance to their relationship despite being surrounded by children. I believe this is one way that couples can both spend some special time alone while setting a wonderful example for the children that their mom and dad really love each other. Of course you don't have to take up drinking hot tea. You can come home and relax over a glass of Coke, cup of coffee, or some other beverage while snacking on cookies or carrot sticks or whatever you prefer.

For parents with small children, it might be impossible to spend quiet time alone until after the children are put to bed. The importance is the uninterrupted time spent together. Whatever means you use to be able to do that consistently is up to you.

Recipe for Romance

Anonymous
Akron, OH

This takes a lot of work, but it's worth it. I went to an antique store and bought an old wooden recipe card box. I took a wood burner and on top of it burned my wife's name and some flowers. Then on the front I wood-burned "Today I love you because . . ."

The first card in the box talked about the age and beauty of the wood, like our marriage. And it promised there were far more reasons I love her than this box could ever hold.

Every day since that day (several months ago) I have made a 4 × 6 card that started with "Today I love you because . . ." Some reasons are funny, some are serious. Some reflect my mood for the day.

Before I leave the house every morning, I leave a card somewhere I know she will find it. Like in the refrigerator, in her car or purse, or hidden in the morning paper.

But this exercise has two very wonderful benefits: 1) It forces me to think hard about why I really do love my wife today. Any man who spends this much time thinking about why he loves his wife will surely start treating her like the treasure she is. 2) It may take a long time, but by golly, she's eventually going to believe you. Just hang in there.

The Question Game

A few weeks back some friends came over for dinner. Afterward we decided to play a game instead of watching a movie. After all, we invited them over to spend time with them, not to stare quietly at the television for two hours together. We weren't in the mood for cards or a board game so we improvised and played "The Question Game." The very simple object of the game is to get to know one another better.

The first two rounds we each took turns telling the others one thing that we liked. Caviar, honest people, hot baths, ice-cream sundaes, helping others succeed, swimming with dolphins, and yellow tulips were some of the comments that were vocalized.

On the third round we each shared with the others one thing we did not like. We opened up to not liking people who make fun of others or who are intolerant of other cultures or beliefs. One person didn't like beans and another found seafood to be repulsive.

While eating dessert and drinking champagne we repeated the cycle until we got bored of playing. The best part was that everyone won. We learned more about one another and became closer friends because of it. This game is also an excellent nonthreatening way to discuss things you don't like that your spouse does. For example, you can

> ### it's the little things:
> ....
> rose petals floating in the water of a
> hot-drawn bath

tell the group that you don't like seeing people talk with food in their mouth or use profanity without pointing the finger. Better yet, it is a way to drop hints about what kind of gifts you would like to receive and how you would spend your ideal romantic day.

Instead of renting that next movie, play a game where everyone wins!

Music to Their Ears

Does the love of your life ever travel without you, either on business or to visit their family? Do you ever wonder if they think of you and miss you when they are away? Here's a way you can guarantee they will think of you and the only cost is the price of one or two blank cassette tapes.

If you want someone to think of you, I can think of no better way than to put your voice on tape. Most of us don't feel comfortable just talking into a microphone without knowing what they are going to say. I suggest reading a book.

Books on tape have become increasingly popular the last few years as people who like to read find they can no longer find the time or they listen to tapes as a productive way to fill up their commuting time.

What you record depends on the tastes of your significant other. My wife would love it if I read *Winnie the Pooh* or *Peter Rabbit* on tape. Others may prefer Shakespeare, Kipling, Stephen Covey, or Gary Smalley.

If you want to be really creative, you could write your own story to read or you could take an existing story and change the names and other details of the book to closely match your life. Just make certain the story has a happy ending.

Once you have recorded the tape, you must decide how you are going to give it to the person for whom you made it. You can mail it in advance to where they will be staying. You can place it in their suitcase or briefcase. If they will be driving, you can pop it in the tape player of the car so it will come on automatically when they start the car. If they will not be in a car, you will need to provide a tape player as well.

The World's Best Mother's Day Present

In the United States we celebrate Mother's Day every May. It is a time to honor our mothers and remind them how special they are to us. Each year many of us wonder what is the best present we can give to our moms.

Without a doubt, the absolutely best present any son can give to his mother is to be a great husband and father. What mother wouldn't love to see her son adoring his wife and treating her like a princess? All women dream of marrying a prince someday. Very few husbands turn out to be princes so the second best thing would be to have your son be the man fairy tales are made of (kind, gentle, understanding, slow to anger, considerate, patient, compassionate, etc.).

When the media calls me the "World's Most Romantic Man" or "Mr. Romance," there isn't a single gift I could buy my mother that would make her happier. The title, indeed, honors my mother. Without her, I would have little concept of what a woman desires in a man. I certainly never learned it from my father or step-father. It was my mother who told me as a teenager that a wife craves two things from her husband: to be told frequently that she is loved, and shown often that she is special.

This Mother's Day, honor your mother by truly loving your wife. In fact, make every day Mother's Day.

Home Romantic Home

If asked to describe what would be a typical romantic occasion, the majority of people would probably give details of a full moon, deserted beach, mountain chalet, or other beautiful place where two people could spend some time alone. It just shows how important the atmosphere or setting is to romance.

Likewise, many people have the opinion that they have to go away to those sorts of places in order to have a romantic evening or weekend. That's simply not practical most of the time. Since we spend more time at home than anywhere else, it stands to reason that we might want to make more of an effort in making our own homes more "romance friendly."

Does your home have a fireplace? How often do you use it? Most fireplaces aren't extremely efficient but they sure do look great. People use fireplaces in their homes now for atmosphere—and not just in the winter. You never know when you'll need a romantic getaway, so always have some firewood around and pinecones on hand to throw in so the fire has a lot of romantic "crackle."

Is there a good supply of candles handy? Turn off the lights, light the candles, and presto! you have a romantic setting. Alladin's genie couldn't have transformed the room any quicker. Also, you might want to consider putting a dimmer on the lights in the dining room. For less than ten dollars you can transform blinding lights into a soft, romantic glow.

Nothing creates a mood quite like music can. You can be in a taxi in the middle of New York City and shut your eyes, put on some soothing music, and instantly it can take your blood pressure down a few notches. So what is "romantic" music? How about a CD or tape of thunder and rain? There are other nature sounds on tape like waves crashing, birds singing, jungle noises, and crickets chirping. They're a nice alternative to the traditional classical music we're accustomed to. Put one of those on and instantly the mood in the room will change.

Invest a little money into making your own home a romantic getaway. It sure beats the expense of going away every weekend just to put a little romance back into your life.

My Dearest Love . . .

The handwritten note or letter is nearly a lost art. In this day of electronic wizardry, it is so simple to send a message nearly instantaneously around the world in just a matter of a few short keystrokes on the computer.

There is still something special about putting a fountain pen to a nice piece of stationery and writing a thank-you card or a letter to a dear friend. It is often therapeutic to not have to use the computer for correspondence.

Women more than men appreciate the gentle art of composing a personalized card or letter. My wife has every imaginable tool that could be used to compose an artful note and she uses them all. If you are in need of a special gift for a dear person, consider a unique box filled with wonderful writing objects. Here are a few suggestions of items you could include:

- Fountain pen
- Different colors of ink
- Sealing-wax sticks
- Sealer (new or antique)
- Nice stationery (maybe personalized)
- Embosser with her name or initials
- LOVE stamps
- Ink blotter
- New or antique desk set

Giving Thanks in Spring

What is your favorite meal of the year? Mine is Thanksgiving.

Why is it that most of us only have the traditional Thanksgiving food during the third and fourth weeks of November? In North America, turkey, cranberry sauce, stuffing, and all the other usual trimmings are available twelve months out of the year.

This year I am determined to have my Thanksgiving meal some time other than in November. What does this have to do with romance, you might be asking? Well, if your man or woman likes turkey and stuffing half as much I do, they would consider it a really, really special occasion if you went all out to prepare the turkey feast.

While you're at it, bring out the good china and crystal for this meal. Make a pumpkin pie. Light the candles. Do just about everything you would normally do on Thanksgiving, especially showing your thanks to the love of your life.

All Work and No Play . . .

I once heard someone describe romance as adult play. I like that concept. I personally believe true romance involves much more play than passion. While passion is important, we often feel "too mature" to have fun. Nonsense!

Those who know me consider me to be one of the biggest kids around. I don't know of any rules that say I can no longer participate in water balloon fights or shoot people with Silly String. I still get excited when I hear the music of the ice-cream truck as it comes into our neighborhood.

Playing is a big part of my wife's and my relationship. Sure, there is always work to be done around the house or in the yard, but living life and enjoying it is so much more important, healthy—and fun. I could spend every waking hour doing paperwork, removing weeds, or cleaning up around the house but I much prefer taking my wife out to eat an ice-cream cone or looking for four-leaf clovers in a big clover patch. When was the last time you did that?

Do you ever walk in the woods or meadows together and pick bouquets of wildflowers? How about playing hide-

and-seek or kick-the-can with your children or the neighborhood kids? When did you last skip rocks on water or race leaves down a stream?

I love to bake cookies with my wife and eat them piping hot out of the oven and drink a big, cold glass of milk. Yum!

Perhaps the media calls me the "World's Most Romantic Man" because I am the world's biggest kid. I think there might be a connection. Is the kid inside you lost? If so, you better go find him. I've gotta go now. I hear the ice-cream truck.

Bathtub Bubbles

Want to hear of a very clever way of giving a bubble bath gift?

First you need to go to a packing store and buy enough Styrofoam peanuts or pellets to fill up a bathtub, at least halfway. By placing the peanuts or pellets (like you would find in bean bag chairs) in the bathtub, you give the illusion of a bubble bath.

Next, you can "float" the gifts on top of the "bubbles." Or, you can buy a rubber duckie and a little sailboat and float those and "sink" the other gifts below for her to find. Maybe you can cap this all off with a line of peanuts from the front door to the bathtub for her to follow.

Wish Upon a Star

Casandra D. Pineheiro
Dallas, TX

On Valentine's Day a few years ago, I bought my husband his own star!

It's from a company called International Star Registry (call 800-282-3333 or visit www.shopsite.com/stars). It costs forty-five dollars to purchase your star and this is what you get: a beautiful certificate that says International Star Registry in purple and gold (looks very classy). The name of the recipient is written in calligraphy along with the coordinates of the star.

Also included is information about your star, as well as directions and a map of how to find it in the night sky! You can choose to have it framed by them as well; however, I chose to take mine to a framing shop. I found a glass frame with no border that fits perfectly and looks great.

Skeptics scoffed at me, "Ha! How can you be sure that it's your star? They could sell the same person the same star a hundred times over!" Well, I tell them, I disagree. With a kazillion stars out there, the company has plenty to choose from.

I know that this is my husband's star. It will be there forever and I can always look up to it and think of him.

Flame Her Heart

Chris Gobble
Salisbury, NC

I am constantly looking for ways to be romantic or for little things to do for my wife. It is a thrill for me to light up that romantic flame in my wife's life.

I had been searching for a way to display my love for her in a public place. One day in the early part of the week she had made plans to go with her best friend to the mall and eat at a cafeteria-type restaurant. I knew this would be the perfect place to leave her roses because of the long line you have to wait on to get your food.

On Saturday I picked out the most beautiful roses I could find. They were white, trimmed with red. I knew the time my wife and her friend were going to eat so I was going to put the roses at the checkout stand where everyone is waiting in line. I took the roses to the mall and made sure they didn't see me leave them. I told the lady at the checkout what my wife was wearing and what she looked like and put her name on the roses.

As my wife and her friend were waiting in line they heard everyone talking about how beautiful the roses were. Who were they for? When my wife got to the checkout she was shocked to find out they were for her.

When she got home she told me the story and I knew romance was flaming in her heart. I had a better time planning and doing it than she did receiving it! Expressing love keeps the flame burning and is a lot of fun.

It's a Wrap

Once a man has bought a gift for his wife or girlfriend, the biggest dilemma is yet ahead: How do I wrap it? I am the first to admit that I don't relish having to wrap gifts. Whenever my wife and I buy presents for friends and family, I ask her to do the wrapping honors.

This is not a step-by-step guide on how to wrap a gift—you wouldn't want directions from me anyway—I am simply giving you some suggestions of unique materials to use to do the wrapping. A creative choice of paper makes up for a sloppy wrapping job.

- A large piece from a brown paper bag (instead of taping it closed, use the sealing wax and sealer that you bought her for her writing box)
- Pages from the Victoria's Secret catalog (good for wrapping lingerie)
- Old wall calendar (for watches/clocks)
- Travel posters (ask a travel agent)
- The Sunday comics
- A personalized picture or artwork created on your computer
- White butcher paper personally decorated with crayons
- Colored plastic wrap
- Greatly enlarged photocopy of a photograph
- Pages of your children's artwork
- Vintage movie posters

Don't Do Dull Dinner Dates

In my observations of the dating scene (of both singles and married couples) the most common date is the dinner date. It's a natural fit, as we all need to eat and no one really enjoys eating alone. Also, going out for dinner takes much less effort than cooking at home.

If you are getting a little bored with the typical dinner date, there are some ways of livening things up. In most medium to large cities there are places where you can go for dinner and enjoy entertainment at the same time.

An example of a unique dining experience is a mystery dinner. Some restaurants invite local actors to perform a murder mystery play in the midst of diners who are supposed to guess "who done it" by the time dessert is served.

Cigar/wine dinners are becoming a booming industry. Some of the finer restaurants are having several-course, pre-planned dinners with different exotic cigars/wines served throughout the evening. You will have to lay out a bit more cash than the average dinner, but they make for a wonderful special occasion.

How about eating a meal while laughing hysterically? If this sounds like fun to you, then you might want to look for a comedy club nearby that serves meals. I would recommend knowing a little about the comedian before you make reservations. Some can be extremely crude, which might not be the type of humor you or your date would enjoy. Dinner and a movie seem to go hand in hand, so dinner theaters are a natural fit. These movie houses usually show second-run films while you are enjoying your meal.

The price of admission is usually much lower than what you would pay to see a newly released film, so it is even less expensive than your average "dinner and a movie" date.

Ninety-Nine Bottles of Treasure in the Water

In the spring and summer we are more likely to have afternoon picnics at the lake or walks in the woods, exploring rivers and streams. Beaches are also a popular destination that time of year. Wouldn't it be neat if you found a bottle with a note in one of those bodies of water?

I remember when I was a kid (many say I still am) I would look all over in hopes of discovering a floating bottle with a message inside. I admit I would still like to find one.

The chances of discovering such a bottle is nearly 100 percent if you plant it there yourself. The idea is for you to hide the bottle where it is unlikely for anyone else to discover it and then take your sweetheart on a picnic or walk for them to "discover" the mysterious bottle in the water.

While any old bottle will do, you might want to shop or rummage around for one that is really interesting or at least would make a nice bud vase. My wife really likes the dark blue wine bottles to put on the table with a few flowers in them. The reason for picking out a nice bottle is that it is likely going to be kept as a memento of the wonderful romantic surprise you pulled off.

What you put inside the bottle is completely up to you. It can be as simple as a love note or as creative as a treasure map (soaked in hot tea and with its edges burned off to make it look aged) that will lead them to a present you have hidden or buried, or even a picnic that you have secretly prepared in the woods or park.

The Odd Couple

Bill Mason
Greenwood, DE

Isn't it interesting? You can sit on one of those benches at the mall for hours and see some of the oddest couples walk by. I have always marveled at how so many of them seem to be mismatched. She is so good-looking and he— well, just isn't. Any observer would have to wonder what his secret is.

Well, I know what it is.

A friend of mine just recently won the serious affections of an extremely good-looking lady. If you could see my friend up close, you would have to agree that he has successfully reached far beyond what anyone ever thought his capabilities might be.

Here is what he did that made the difference. At least, this is what she told me.

This lady has been wined and dined by the best of them. It has almost become mundane for her: a good-looking guy, a nice restaurant, excellent food, small talk, holding hands, and then the usual invitation to find some place where they could "have a nice time together." She was fed up with the meaningless relationships based solely on appearances and physical attraction.

Then my friend came along. He asked her if she would like to have Chinese take-out for dinner. Can you believe that? Then he told her that he had written a song for her. Well, he is no songwriter and his guitar playing is less than great, but he put a lot of work into his little musical presentation and his sincerity impressed her.

She consented.

What was amazing is that she agreed to meet him at his apartment. He had set his table up with a lit candle in the center, a bottle of wine, two glasses, and several little white cartons containing Chinese food from a local restaurant. At first she wondered what he had in mind, but his genuine, sweet demeanor made her feel that she could trust him. They ate and talked for a while. Then my friend played his guitar and sang his little song for her. He is no Neil Diamond, but she was absolutely taken by his effort in this regard. They chatted for hours afterward.

Now, here is what did the trick.

As the evening progressed, she kept wondering when he was going to make a move on her. Well, it never happened. As the hour grew late, they decided to call it an evening and he walked her to the door of her car. She said she just had to at least kiss him good-bye, so she did.

She called him the next night and told him that no man has ever done that for her before, not ever. They are now seeing each other regularly and it is obvious that it is becoming very serious.

My friend is just an average-looking guy. If you saw the two of them walking together in the mall you would really wonder what it is that this guy has to attract a woman as gorgeous as she is.

It's simple. His approach to romance assures her that it is the person inside that he cares about more than anything else. A woman needs to feel cherished and he knew that.

Now whenever I take a few moments to sit in the mall and do some people watching, I know why the above-average-looking ladies have their arms around below-average-looking guys.

Looks are important, but not as much as connecting to a woman's soul as far as the female of the species is concerned. Smart, below-average-looking guys should know that.

People Watching People

Who doesn't like to people watch? People come in all shapes, sizes, and colors. I love the variety.

Sometimes Athena and I will make a game out of people watching. We take turns picking someone out of the crowd and telling their story. We explain their background, what their ambitions are, and why they're at this mall/coffee shop/park.

For example: "That lady over there in the turban was once an eastern European aristocrat. She left her homeland to search for her long-lost boyfriend, who was rumored to

be living in South America. She packed up her bags and
cats and headed for Venezuela, but the boat capsized. She
and her cats were rescued by the U.S. Navy, and she liked
America so much she decided to stay. Now she is an inte-
rior decorator and is at the mall looking for some plastic
eggs she can decorate to look like the Fabergé eggs."

We each take turns telling tales to entertain and humor
the other. Sometimes the stories are very realistic, other
times they are quite farfetched, but they are always fun.

Chalk It Up!

I discovered the most wonderful romantic tool the other
day—glow-in-the-dark chalk! I have been having a lot of fun
with it. I wrote some welcome-home messages to my wife
on our front sidewalk. My sidewalk "art" shows up day or
early night (the glowing properties only last an hour or so
after it is no longer exposed to light).

Next, I drew hearts and wrote silly messages all over our
white bedroom walls. The graffiti is impossible to see in the
daytime, but at night it shows up faintly (the fatter and
larger drawings show up better). Athena got a big kick out
of it when she turned off the lights and she saw glowing
hearts and sentimental messages surrounding the bed.
Cleanup was a piece of cake. All I had to do was turn off
the lights and I knew exactly where to scrub the walls.

I find glow-in-the-dark stars to be much brighter, but the chalk is quite versatile and creative. Chalk one up to romance!

Calling All Friends, Family, and Celebrities

On May 27, 1997, Athena and I celebrated our seventh yearly wedding anniversary. I wanted to make it even more special than our average yearly extravaganza, so I came up with an idea to make it very memorable. I wanted to have friends, family, and celebrities send greetings to Athena to congratulate her on this special occasion.

First, about one month before our anniversary, I went on the Internet and found several sites where celebrity mailing addresses were listed. I wrote down about twenty-five celebrities around the world that Athena has admired for things they have accomplished or talents they have. I didn't write to anyone simply because they were good-looking or famous. I did my best to hunt down a few more addresses of notables that I knew of whom Athena was particularly fond. I wrote each person a short letter explaining what I was doing. Along with the letter I included a card and envelope that was preaddressed and stamped so all they would have to do is to write a short note, sign it, seal it, and post it. About two weeks before our anniversary, the card from Woody Allen came. In proper fashion, Martha Stewart's came just a few days before our anniversary. On the day of our anniversary came greetings from Brooke Shields, Andre Aggasi, and Harry Connick Jr. Within the next few weeks came cards from Bill Cosby, Robin Williams, Emma Thompson, and the cast of *Friends*.

The second tier of this plan had to do with friends and family who have e-mail. I sent messages to about forty people who have e-mail and asked them to send a message to my wife at her office. The day of our anniversary (she had to work, unfortunately), she was flooded with dozens of messages over the computer. The reason I didn't ask our friends to send a card is that it would have been expensive for me to send out an additional forty requests, and it would have been slightly rude to ask for them to go out and buy a card for us.

I did make Athena something special in celebration of our seventh anniversary. Keep reading and you will find out what it was.

Toss Her a Bouquet

Flowers are romantic. Everyone knows that. However, not all flowers are created equal.

A dozen roses are not as romantic as a hand-picked bouquet given "just because." Tulips are not as romantic as daisies if daisies are actually her favorite flower. I believe the most romantic flowers of all are the ones she included in her wedding bouquet.

If there is a special occasion or anniversary on the horizon, consider presenting her with a bouquet of flowers just like the ones she carried down the aisle. Just go sifting through your wedding album for a photo of her bridal bouquet. Make a photocopy of the picture and take it along with the original to a florist so they can re-create the arrangement your bride held on your very special day. Let the florist look at the original picture for clarity and then let them keep the photocopy as they assemble the arrangement. Be sure to safely return the original photograph back into the album.

Present the bouquet to your bride and watch the tears flow. There are some florists that can freeze-dry the bouquet so it will last for years to come.

If you want to pull out all the stops, you can also have the top layer of your wedding cake re-created and find the music that played at the ceremony.

Want Romance, Learn to Dance

One of the biggest crazes of these past few years has been ballroom and swing dancing. Around the country classes are filling up almost as soon as new ones are added. Young and old alike are yearning for the simplistic romance of yesteryear: dancing.

Many people are tiring of the loud modern dance clubs where they come home with ringing in their ears and smelling like stale cigarette smoke. They are looking for a place where you can actually talk with your dance partner and even hold them close.

While the majority of women jump at the chance of doing some real dancing, most men are a bit more reserved, if not fearful of the idea. I would imagine this is because they are afraid of looking foolish out there on the dance floor.

Dancing lessons are the ideal solution to anyone's ballroom phobias. You will be just as awkward and out of step as the person learning next to you. But in a few weeks' time, as you learn to gently hold your sweetheart and graciously dip her out of your arms, you will make her the envy of every woman.

A Toast to Seven Years

Within six months of our marriage, I had already broken both of our engraved toasting glasses. Every time we go to drink champagne, I am reminded of what a klutz I was.

When it came to giving Athena an anniversary gift on our seventh anniversary, those crystal champagne glasses came back to mind. However, we already have some champagne glasses and really don't need any more. What Athena had been wanting was a nice glass juice pitcher that could also be used as a water pitcher for when we have company over. Also, we have had several Mexican dinners recently and have wished we had proper margarita glasses for those killer strawberry margaritas I make.

A few weeks ago I was delighted to see a margarita pitcher and glass set on sale. Without Athena knowing, I bought the set and then went to a craft store and bought some etching paste and etching stencils.

When she was off at work one day, I decorated the glasses with leftover glow-in-the-dark stars I had lying around. I then put the etching paste all over the glass (using gloves and a Popsicle stick) and let it sit for five minutes before rinsing. After rinsing, I removed the stars and the result was nicely frosted glasses except where the stars had been.

For the pitcher I applied the etching stencils of moons, stars, and etching letters to spell out a message (what it says is my secret and I'm not sharing). I put the etching paste just over the stencils and letters and let it sit for two minutes, per the directions, and then washed it all away. The result was amazingly professional looking. Now instead of having two itty-bitty toasting glasses, we have one huge toasting pitcher. I would say we upgraded.

Why I Tried to Kill My Wife

My wife shot me the other day. It's okay. I tried to kill her first. She was just acting in self-defense.

With several of our friends, Athena and I tried out the game of paintball. It is a game created by some farmers who had originally been using paintball guns to mark which cows needed to be vaccinated. They brilliantly came up with the idea of making a military-type game with the guns. In the last few years, it has grown into a multibillion-dollar industry.

We began the day with a game of capture-the-flag. Athena and I were on the same team and we managed to steal the other team's flag and bring it back to our home base for the victory. In a different game where Athena shot me, she was originally on my team but the other team shot her so she had to defect to their team. When she shot me, I also had to join their team so we were back together again.

Perhaps you are scratching your head by now and wondering what this has to do with romance. There is no greater romance than between a couple who are best friends. And friendships are based on shared experiences. Paintball is just one more unique experience that Athena and I have shared together that has bound us even closer. The next time you feel like killing your spouse, go play some paintball.

No Fat but All the Fun

For Secretary's Day, my wife received a box of assorted Jelly Bellys. For those who aren't familiar with these candies, they are miniature jelly beans that come in dozens of flavors: mint, orange, pineapple, coffee, tutti-frutti, peach,

leaving a loving message on your spouse's voice
mail at night so they will hear your voice first
thing in the morning when they arrive at work

cotton candy, buttered popcorn, and root beer, to name just
a few.

While sampling my wife's gift I thought of a fun game to
play with the Jelly Bellys. You can either buy the assortment
pack or go to a candy or specialty grocery store where they
are sold and buy a few of each flavor.

The basic concept of the game is a blindfolded taste test.
One person is blindfolded while the other feeds them various
flavors. For each flavor guessed correctly, they win a
prize (a kiss, a five-minute massage, a one-minute back
scratch, etc.). For each flavor guessed incorrectly, they lose
a prize (or have to give the other person a prize). To make
it a little easier, you can give the person two chances to
guess the flavor. If they get it on the first try, they get a
better prize than if they guess it on the second.

To make the game even more interesting, you can combine Jelly Bellys to make unique flavors. Root beer and vanilla together creates a root beer float. Coconut and
pineapple combine to make a piña colada. Chocolate and
cherry ones create a chocolate-covered cherry. There are at
least a dozen different combinations that can be made from
the nearly one hundred flavored Jelly Bellys. Perhaps you
can have a different scoring system for combination flavors.

You can buy dozens of Jelly Bellys for just a dollar, and
best of all, they contain no fat. Don't worry about any cal-

ories. You will work them off when it is time to redeem your prizes.

Peek-a-boo Pajamas

Paul Arnold
Auburn, MI

One thing I have started to do is to fold my wife's pajamas and put them under her pillow. I usually do this while she's in the shower or after she's left for her kindergarten class. She says when she gets ready for bed at night and lifts the pillow and sees her pajamas folded it makes her feel special. She is!

(Author's note: Besides putting pajamas under the pillow, you can place mints, rose petals, wrapped chocolates, hand-written cards, or other special treats. If you go the chocolate route make certain the candy is discovered or else you'll have a big mess on your hands the next morning. This extra bit of attention will make for some very pleasant dreams.)

What to Give?

Some people can be so hard to shop for. I am one of them. I don't enjoy most traditional gifts. I don't know the reason. Maybe it is because I am creative. Maybe it is because I am just weird. But I do know I'm not alone.

Here are some suggestions of gifts that I would like and maybe so would someone else who is difficult to shop for.

- Nicely framed baby pictures of me and of my wife
- A big bag of root beer barrel candies
- A twenty-minute back scratch
- Dinner at a murder mystery cafe
- A large batch of fresh oatmeal-raisin cookies
- Seeing a live taping of *Friends*
- An afternoon playing paintball
- An entire day of rest and pampering
- An ice-cream banana split/sundae with *everything* on it
- Someone to wax my car
- A day at a water park, amusement park, or arcade
- A surprise picnic at a unique location

(Sure is a lot of food on this list!)

Showing Your Love the Write Way

Lori Stidham
Rosyln, PA

Here is one way I like to express my love for my husband. Any man or woman can do this, and for a man who thinks he could never write poetry, it's much easier than you might think.

Our local newspaper holds a Valentine contest every year

and I take full advantage of it! I love the feeling I get creating my poem, the feeling I get waiting a few weeks to see if the paper chose my poem as a winner, and finally the feeling I get when Todd opens the paper and sees what I wrote for him.

The easiest way to create a poem is to simply write down events, special moments, feelings, and phrases. Just scribble them down in any order on a blank sheet of paper. I like to flip through photo albums and let the pictures inspire me and I jot down a few words about special photos. I also read other bits of poetry to get my mind thinking in a "rhyming" way. I make little lists of words that rhyme with the key words I want to use and before I know it, the lines begin to form.

The poems bring smiles to my husband's face, not to mention the faces of friends and family! Even neighbors recognize our names in the paper and compliment us! My husband is very proud.

We frame the newspaper clippings and hang them up. I smile to myself when I see my husband stop to read a poem he's read a hundred times.

Wanted: Mental Editor

Do you practice mental editing? What is that, you ask? The most common problem we humans get ourselves into is speaking before we think. Our words have separated best friends, divorced once-close couples, and have even brought countries to war against each other.

I like to practice what I term "mental editing." If I have the chance, I try to speak to myself in my head and see how it sounds before I verbalize it to others. Sometimes I simply rearrange words in my head so the thought will be clearer. There are many times I completely erase those sentences before they have the chance to come out of my mouth. After going over it in my head I realized what I was about to say was irrelevant or was going to be something that I would later regret.

Nowadays, we often write our letters on a word processor. We have the opportunity to go back and edit what we have written. We change things because when we reread it, it is obvious that perhaps it might be taken the wrong way or may be slightly hurtful or even come across as being arrogant.

If you have the chance, formulate your thoughts in your mental word processor and edit them before you begin to speak—especially on delicate topics.

Playing with Your Food

Food sure is fun. It is fun to eat and, despite what my mother tried to teach me, it is fun to play with. Have you ever played with your food? Try it, you might like it.

One particularly fun food is hearty toast and eggs. Take two slices of bread and use a heart cookie cutter to take a hole out of the center of one piece. Lightly toast both pieces. Scramble up an egg and just when it begins to take some nonrunny form, put the toast in the skillet and place the eggs in the open heart of the bread for it to finish cooking. Serve with grits, bacon, or some other side dish.

You can alter the above idea for even a simple peanut butter and jelly sandwich. Place the piece of bread with the heart cut out on top of a whole slice. Does your lover like licorice? A message written in licorice "string" might just brighten their day.

If you are creating a Chinese meal or ordering one in, that would be the perfect occasion to make a giant fortune cookie with a special poem or note tucked inside. I'll even provide the recipe.

My mom knows I still play with my food, but now she gives her approval.

GIANT FORTUNE COOKIES

1 cup all-purpose flour
2 tablespoons cornstarch
$^1/_2$ cup sugar
$^1/_2$ teaspoon salt
$^1/_2$ cup vegetable oil
$^1/_2$ cup egg whites (whites of about 4 large eggs)
1 tablespoon water
2 tablespoons vanilla extract

Prepare fortune, poem, or note to include in cookies. Cut or fold the paper so it is approximately 1" × 3" in size.

Mix all the dry ingredients and then add oil and egg whites until smooth; beat in water and vanilla extract.

Drop $^1/_3$ cup of batter onto a greased baking sheet and spread evenly into a 10-inch circle.

Bake only one or two at a time in a preheated, 300-degree oven for about 14 minutes or until light golden brown; if underbaked, cookies will tear during shaping.

With a wide spatula, remove one cookie at a time from the oven. Working quickly, flip it onto your hand (please use a towel or oven mitt, or wear cotton gloves). Place fortune in center of cookie and fold it in half, but do not crease it. Then fold the two ends toward each other and hold for a minute or two while it hardens. Repeat until all the batter is used. Makes 6 cookies.

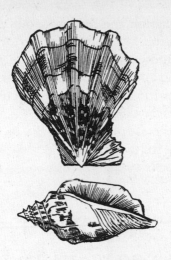

Sunsets, Sand Castles, and Seashells

A couple of summers ago Athena and I went camping with some friends on the beach. In the morning one friend stepped out of her tent and saw "I love you" written by her husband with seashells in the sand. He made a special effort to wake up early to gather the shells and arrange them for her.

Some people think the only thing romantic about beaches is the sunrises or sunsets. Those should be only the beginning or ending of a romantic day on the sand.

How about having a sand castle competition? If you are traveling with other friends like we were, you and your love can work together on your creation. Remember, romance is having fun. It's not all about smooching (well, that can be fun too).

Next at the beach you can comb for seashells after high tide has washed new ones ashore. If you are allowed to remove them from the beach, take them home and clean them in diluted bleach and they will forever remind you of the fun you had finding them.

If fires are permitted, build one to make s'mores (roasted-marshmallow and chocolate bar on a graham cracker). Then snuggle up under the stars while you sip mint-flavored hot chocolate or your favorite hot drink.

To finish off the evening, tell stories or play The Question Game (see page 65) around the fire.

Summer Blizzards

In the heat of the summer I just crave ice cream. Fortunately, there is a Dairy Queen about a mile from our house. Some evenings, Athena and I walk to the DQ, as it is affectionately nicknamed. Often we have coupons we have clipped for a free blizzard (soft ice cream with wonderful candy bars or other items mixed in) or two-for-one sundae.

This simple walk has several benefits. First, the ice cream satisfies my cravings and tastes so good when it is hot and humid outside. It is a fairly inexpensive treat and I think it is very important to pamper ourselves every once in a while. The walk is great exercise even if we are going to put the pounds back on as soon as we down our blizzards. We could drive there, but then we wouldn't get any physical benefit. Most important is the time Athena and I have together as we walk. On the way there and between mouthfuls on the way back, we have some really wonderful conversations.

Is there an ice-cream shop, snowball stand, or video rental place just a mile or two from your house? How about walking together as you go to indulge yourself? It's worth the walk and it's worth the wait.

Let's Do Lunch

Is the only time you spend with your sweetheart during the work week those few hours after coming home from work and before going to bed? And are those hours taken up by fixing dinner, doing chores, and running errands?

If at all possible, do lunch with your love.

Fortunately, my wife and I worked for the same corporation for many years and we were able to have lunch together several times a week. It was great to connect in the middle of the day and just talk. Sometimes we talked about things we needed to do at home or talked about work, but often we'd just talk about fun things. We discussed what we wanted to do with our lives, the kind of dream home we would like to have, and what we thought about different world issues. On top of that, nearly every afternoon around three o'clock, Athena would come up to my office for a fifteen-minute afternoon break and I would make us each a cup of hot tea. I would usually have a couple of cookies or a piece of candy there too, and she referred to them as her afternoon "treats." It was a special time we looked forward to every day.

Of course, most couples do not work in such close proximity to be able to have an afternoon break together, but many couples could certainly get together for lunch more often than they do. If you don't have time (or the money) to go to a restaurant for lunch, brown-bag it.

If it's not possible to meet for lunch, have a "phone date" at lunch. Even ten minutes talking on the phone at lunch will make a marked improvement in each of your afternoons.

The next time either of you complain that you don't get to spend enough quality time together, suggest, "Let's do lunch."

Look for Things That Go Bang in the Night

Last weekend I took Athena to see a movie at the local museum of art's outdoor movie night. The admission was $2.50 and we packed a picnic dinner to eat before the film began.

Summer is full of free or very cheap outdoor activities. Concerts in the park, street festivals, battle reenactments, fireworks displays, outdoor plays, and other delightful events fill the pages of community calendars each summer. Keep your eyes peeled for these fantastic (and cheap) dates for you and your sweetheart. If you bring children along, they will be so mesmerized with the excitement that you will be able to steal a few kisses without them noticing. If they do "catch you," it might set a great example for them when they are your age.

Welcome Your Honey Home

When I was in grade school, I was often so anxious for my mom or dad to come home that I would wait down at the end of the block, looking eagerly for their car to come down the street. I also remember the excitement of hearing the car pull up into the driveway and racing outside to greet them with a big hug and perhaps help them unload items from the car.

Are you ever excited to see your sweetheart come home? Do you show it? Or has it simply become some part of a monotonous routine?

There are many other ways of letting him or her know you are glad to see them. Of course, waiting at the end of the block is the ultimate in flattery (with a bouquet of flowers—that would really get their hearts racing or wondering what you broke). Here are some more:

- Make a special drink for their arrival.
- Have their favorite CD playing.
- Come out of the house and greet them at the car, helping with any packages.
- Greet them at the door with a kiss and a hug.
- As soon as they come in, sit them down, take off their shoes, and rub their feet.
- Write a welcome-home note on the sidewalk with chalk.
- Present them with a small gift, "just because."

Why I Want to Beat Up (Paper) Animals

I have one disappointment in life. I have never been able to bust up a piñata and have candies and prizes fall all over me.

I have witnessed them in real life and I have seen them on television shows and in the movies. I just never personally experienced the thrill of being showered with cool treats. I might also enjoy being a bystander who swoops in when the break is made and the person with the stick is still blindfolded and disoriented.

One doesn't have to go with the traditional "party piñata." It can also be made clear that what is inside doesn't have to be shared. A piñata would be a wonderful addition to an adult birthday party, an anniversary celebration, or a way to give a Christmas present. Just think of the items you could put in a piñata (besides an engagement ring box). Here are a few examples (nothing breakable of course).

♦ Sports theme: tickets to a game, baseball cards, peanuts.
♦ Cracker Jack theme: candied popcorn and silly prizes like plastic animals and fake tattoos.
♦ Turning-forty theme: Fix-o-Dent, hair dye, arthritis pills, Ex-Lax.
♦ Chocolate theme: An assortment of wrapped chocolates and packets of hot chocolate.

Two Forks, Two Knives, One Plate

Have you ever watched *Lady and the Tramp*? If I ask you what is the first thing that comes to mind, you probably would say the scene where the two dogs are sharing a plate of spaghetti.

There is no doubt about it, food is romantic. It amplifies the senses and fulfills one of our deepest needs. There are certain types of food that are romantic by nature: chocolate, strawberries, and small pastries, for example. Then there are foods that are romantic because of the atmosphere: surrounded by candles, elegant music playing in the background, or served on a linen-covered table with a vase of fresh flowers.

Who would have thought that a plate of spaghetti could be so romantic? But Lady and the Tramp showed us that sharing one plate is a perfect way to be united with each other. Have you ever eaten off the same plate as your love? How often do you feed each other? When was the last time you shared a strand of spaghetti or a baby corn and ended in a kiss?

Everyone has to eat. But not everyone has to have their own plate.

Designing a Really Cool Book Cover

It is amazing how much thought someone will put into picking out the perfect present yet use very little imagination on how to give it. In many ways, the presentation of a gift is just as important as the item itself. Imagine buying someone a gold ring and leaving it on the kitchen counter with a note that says, "Thought you might like this." Or contrast that with the gift of a ring hidden inside a rosebud that will "magically" appear as the rose blossoms in the sunlight.

The next time you are giving a gift, consider presenting

it in a creative or meaningful way. I will give a few examples of things I have done which I hope will spur your own
creative juices to flow and come up with ideas on your
own. Of course I am flattered when my ideas are mimicked;
however, I know that I am not the sole romantic person
on earth. My aim is to bring out the romantic that is inside
each of you.

On one Saturday morning while my wife was sleeping
in late I ran a string all through the house, beginning at the
location where I hid her gift. The string went through cab-
inets, under seat cushions, in the bathtub, behind the sofa,
and throughout all the rooms in the house. Had I been
thinking ahead, I would have attached small gifts all along
the string as a teaser for the big present at the end. After I
ran the string through our home, I brought the other end
of the string to my wife in bed and explained that I had
bought a present for her and it was at the other end. I had
never seen her get out of bed so quickly on a Saturday
morning.

Another way in which I like to give presents to my wife
is by having her trace clues to find them. I will write about
seven or so clues which lead from one written clue to the
next until the final clue leads to the hidden gift. Sometimes
I will even write the clues in the form of poetry. Here is an
example:

> With your ear you'll hear
> Not the ocean or the sea
> But the next clue telling you
> Where the treasure trove will be.
> (The next clue was inside a conch shell.)

If you want to go all out on the "treasure hunt" theme, you
can give your spouse a tape in the *Mission Impossible* style,
giving them their assignment to locate the missing gift. Depending on the time you have and equipment available, you

can even include videotaped clues, which definitely would add to the overall excitement of the quest.

Once I created a treasure hunt through town which ended in a park where she had to walk certain paces to find where her "treasure" lay. This time it was a picnic that I prepared in advance and asked a friend to lay out for us while we were finding our way there.

There are dozens and dozens of ways in which you can transform the presentation of even an ordinary gift into a truly romantic occasion. Remember that regardless of what people say, books are judged by their cover.

Great Ball of Fire

Holidays and special anniversaries are wonderful reminders for romance. However, they are also the most predictable. A small but meaningful gesture on an "ordinary day" often has more impact than a larger investment on an "expected day."

One way to encourage spontaneous romance is with a friendship ball/box. Find a nice, small hollow ball or box. It is important that it can be opened and shut.

The friendship ball is almost like a "hot potato." You are supposed to put a little treasure inside and place it for your love to find. Then it is their turn to fill it up and give it back to you. The intention is for there to be a never-ceasing exchange of tokens of love.

You might choose to place the ball inside the refrigerator with a hand-picked flower or a piece of luscious chocolate inside. It could be returned to your pillow with tickets to the theater or a favorite comic strip. The exchange could possibly go on indefinitely. Regardless of whether it does or not, the romance in your relationship will hopefully always be on fire.

Boyfriends, Husbands, Lend Me Your Ears

Jennifer Stephens
Richardson, TX

My husband of three years has worked really hard at developing and maintaining his romantic side during our marriage. He is affectionate and considerate and does his best to make me feel loved every day. However, he generally thinks most things that a woman would consider romantic to be "sappy" and not really necessary. He can handle flowers on our anniversary and the occasional grand gesture, but day-to-day romantic gestures he views as superfluous. That is why this small event was so special to me.

Kevin, like most other men I know, has a low tolerance for talking about feelings. As a computer sales engineer he is in the business of solving people's problems rather than listening to them talk about them. I call this his "Mr. Fix-It" syndrome. "Mr. Fix-It," however, does not always translate well to relationships. Like other women I know, if I am upset about something, my first priority is to air my bad feelings and to feel understood. Kevin's first priority is to give advice and solve the problem. If he cannot do that, he feels powerless and frustrated. Thus, we often feel like we are speaking different languages even if we have the same goal.

After Kevin endured a four-hour flight home from a week-long business trip last week, we went out to dinner. I had recently taken on a new job and was feeling overwhelmed and not really up to the challenge. Thus, we were both exhausted and grouchy.

I hadn't planned on telling him how frustrated I was, but it all spilled out at once. Kevin tried to offer me solutions right and left, but I just wanted to be heard. I grew more and more quiet, not even realizing yet that I hadn't wanted advice but rather had wanted to be understood. To his credit, Kevin figured out on his own and subtly switched to telling me that he understood how I felt. He put aside his own exhaustion and his need to be "Mr. Fix-It" and attended to my feelings.

All of a sudden, my frustration faded away in the face of his caring attentiveness. He thinks I didn't notice, but I did and I know how hard it was for him to do. I think it is one of the most romantic things he has ever done for me, and it didn't cost nearly as much as dinner!

Bring Out the Tiger in Her

I received a newsletter in the mail announcing that our favorite recording artist, Loreena McKennitt, was releasing her new album on September 30. Her albums are the only ones we "collect." She calls her style world music. It is an amazing blend of folk sounds from around the world accompanied by her heavenly voice.

Loreena travels around the globe, researching people and their cultures, and paints the experiences into her music. It is both moving and thought provoking. For Athena and me, it is romantic. It is often the chosen music for our candle-light dinners or our evenings of snuggling on the sofa, drinking hot chocolate.

I knew Athena would be delighted to hear her new CD. While she was at work, I purchased the album and created a trail from our front door all the way into our office. The trail included Loreena's newsletter, some old fliers, and the CD cases of her other six albums we own.

When I heard Athena open the front door, I began playing the album on my computer (yes, CD-ROMs can play regular compact discs) to continue to "lure" her to my office. When she had collected all the Loreena memorabilia and finally made it to my desk, she was beaming from ear to ear.

I could have simply bought the CD and handed it to her with a bow on top, but the few extra minutes of thought and time elevated the gift from "that's great" to "that's ggrrrrrrrrrrreeeaaaatt!!!!!!!"

How About a Picnic—Your Place or Mine?

Kevin M. Lydy
Springfield, OH

My intentions were to provide Jenn with a splendid afternoon complete with a picnic. We would drive out to this nice, secluded field I knew of that rested on the outskirts of town. There were rolling hills all around and the view from this particular spot, though not what one would call breathtaking, certainly outdid the day-to-day views of downtown buildings and street corners.

We were to leave around 3:00 in the afternoon, so the sun was going to be out and there would be no need for a jacket. This is what was *supposed* to happen.

The day before we were to have our picnic, Jenn called to tell me she had to go home to visit with her ill grandmother (yes, she really was ill). At first I was crushed, but I was determined to follow through with my intentions, even if the way they would be carried out would be slightly different. She did not have to leave until 2:00, so I decided to have her over for about a half hour or so in order to try and salvage the remnants of my idea.

I made sandwiches, had sparkling champagne (Asti, if you can call that champagne), and tortes for dessert. I placed all of the food items in a picnic basket.

Now, as I said, we did not have the time to go on a picnic, so I decided to have the picnic at my place. I borrowed a green blanket from my friend and draped it over the couch and down onto the floor. I turned one of my fans on low and had it oscillating across the blanket to simulate the gentle breeze that we would have outside. Finally, I put on some baroque music for atmosphere. I went to pick up Jenn and brought her back to my place.

The smile on her face when I opened the door to our "picnic" will forever be in my memory. I was determined to give Jenn a decent afternoon; her smile told me I had succeeded.

Gone Fishin'

Is your relationship tumultuous at times? Maybe you should go fishing.

A recent survey noted several interesting conclusions

about fish owners versus the fishless couples. Did you know that fish owners are *four* times more likely than non-fish owners to characterize their relationship with their mate as "loving, like June and Ward Cleaver from *Leave It to Beaver*"? The survey also shows that nonfish owners are more than twice as likely to suffer from high blood pressure than fish owners. Other symptoms more prevalent in non-fish owners are stress, heart disease, depression, and headaches.

Fish owners are far less likely to be problem drinkers, eaters, and sleepers. On the other hand, I don't think just any pet will have the same results. I have seen many couples fight constantly over dogs and other pets. They argue about who will take the dogs out for walks and who will clean up after the animals. They can cause marital stress if they damage furniture and bring about expensive vet bills. Certain types of pets make it difficult to go away on a romantic weekend. If you are looking to enrich your relationship with a family pet, give fish a try. You can't hold them but they won't keep you up all night with their noises either.

Game of Romance

Is there a puzzle lover in your house? Not the jigsaw type, but crosswords, word searches, and Jumble.

Have you ever made them a personalized word puzzle? Just think of the fun you could have coming up with words that have symbolism and meaning to your relationship. You could put in the name of the first restaurant you had dinner at together, a city where you had a romantic getaway or pet names you have for each other. How about your favorite color, author, or flavor of ice cream?

For more obscure words and clues, search through old photo albums and scrap books. There are bound to be dozens of ideas that will come to mind. The photos might help you remember details of your first kiss or a special item someone wore on the honeymoon. The name of your first pet and street of your first apartment will bring back memories.

The puzzle will be more than a personalized gift. It will be a way to help both of you remember some very wonderful moments of your past and perhaps rekindle that passion that was present in the early years.

Buried Treasure

It's been about twenty years since I got together with a group of neighborhood kids to create a time capsule. To be honest, I don't remember what's in it, but I do remember exactly where we buried it. It was on top of a four-foot hill in the Scheers' backyard, just two doors down from where my mom still lives.

The Scheers no longer live there but each time I visit home I keep meaning to ask the new neighbors down the street if I can go dig in their yard. It sure would be exciting to unearth the box and look to see what items we decided to contribute twenty years ago. I imagine I would get a good laugh at what we thought was interesting or "cool" two decades ago. I am sure it would bring back lots of fond memories too.

It's never too late to create your own time capsule, whether you're twenty, forty, sixty, eighty, or one hundred (though a centenarian might be pushing it a little). I think it would be interesting if couples would bury a capsule right before their wedding and dig it up on their twenty-fifth anniversary. You could include a newspaper from the day you were married as well as many other mementos. Or bury it in the backyard of the first house you buy and wait a decade or so before you dig it up.

One very important element would be the map. No matter how good your memory is now, it is not guaranteed to be reliable in the future. You can create the map in the "pirate's treasure" style or just an ordinary plotting map would be effective too. Come to think of it, I hope that hill in the Scheers' backyard is still there. Of course, as a short ten-year-old, an ant pile might be considered a hill. We should have drawn a map.

Real Men Do Sew

M. John
Centreville, VA

My macho boyfriend recently gave me the most romantic gift . . . curtains. They're romantic to me because of the deep thought behind them and the preparation that went into making them. You see, he came to my house late one night and observed that one could in fact see through the blinds of my window. I thought the blinds were enough and no one could see in the window. I was wrong. He was concerned. So, he went to the fabric store and picked out fabric that matched the colors in my bedroom. He could have easily just *bought* the curtains. But no, he wanted to make them. Of course, that was more special to me. This great guy spent a Friday night making my drapes. Since he is such a perfectionist, he first ironed the fabric. As I watched him with needle and thread while he hemmed the final seams, his attempt at domesticity couldn't have been more sexy or romantic. The show of concern and the thought that went into these drapes are always remembered when I look up at them. And they turned out really good! Too good on that first morning . . . I *overslept* because I wasn't used to the amount of light cut off by my drapes. So, that's my great boyfriend. Though his friends aren't supposed to know he can actually sew. It's just not macho, right?

When Scavengers Become Poets

Michael Wayne
Butler, PA

I was going to be away from home for a week on a business trip, and knew about it several months ahead of time. With that amount of time available, I took about fifteen to thirty minutes a night, three to four nights a week to work on a series of poems. The subject of each poem was, of course, some aspect of my wife that I love. By the time of the trip, I had written a series of fourteen poems about ten to fourteen verses each, with a clue at the end of each poem. Each clue told where my wife could find the next poem in the series. I hid the poems all over the city we live, in places that my wife knew and could deduce easily from the clues. I even gave one to her mom and one to her boss. Also, to be a little more romantic, I used parchment for the poems and I found some wax seals and a stamp with the first letter of my name to seal the poems. Some locations were outside, so I used a sandwich bag to place those. The night before I left, I placed the first poem on her desk at work (we work for the same company). It only took her four days to find all the poems, but it made the time I had to be away fly for both of us. She was busy anticipating the words of the next poem, while I got to listen to her excited words when I called her each night. I also had a very welcome reception when I came home at the end of the week.

This idea is pretty ambitious, and there were some times when I didn't think I could come up with another word, but it was worth every minute I spent.

How to TP Her and Not Get in Trouble

Who ever thought toilet paper could be romantic? I never gave it much thought myself until the other day when one of those crazy ideas popped into my head. I don't even remember what triggered the thought, but I went into my wife's bathroom armed with a black pen and a mission.

I unrolled about a hundred feet of the toilet paper and began writing little messages on the paper and rolled it back up for five feet and wrote another message until there were fifteen or so on the roll. The messages were simple, nothing complicated, nothing too flowery. Just little thoughts to let

> ### it's the little things:
> ···
> making a photocopy of your hand and mailing or
> faxing it to your love at work so they can "hold
> your hand" while you are apart

Athena know I was thinking of her and that she is very special to me.

She was surprised when the first message came around the roll. And then amazed when the second, third, and fourth ones showed up. She even admitted to me that she wouldn't go to the bathroom in the middle of the night because she didn't want to accidentally miss one of my notes. Women sure are funny—and sensitive. Guess that's why we guys love them so much.

If you really adore your wife (or husband), perhaps you should consider toilet-papering them.

Organized Is Not a Romantic Crime

Angela Sutherland
Prince Edward Island, Canada

Here are two ideas on being an organized romantic.

1.) I keep a binder with twelve pocket dividers (one for each month of the year). I put a small card or pocket note in each pocket to send to my boyfriend. The cards may be store-bought or homemade but the idea is just to have a card on hand to let my boyfriend know I am thinking about him.

2.) Being a hopeless romantic, I tend to buy numerous books on romantic ideas. Because the books are filled with a few good ideas that I would never be able to remember in a crunch, I purchased a small file box, some index cards, and dividers (total cost about six dollars). Now when I read an idea I like, I write it on a cue card with the page and book I copied it from and place it in the box under the corresponding category. Some categories I have are: Things to Make, Romantic Ideas, To Do Together, Love Quotes (great for notes or cards), Food Ideas. These are just a few ideas to get you started. Once I use the idea, I write the date I used it and place it at the back of the box to be used at a later date.

(Author's note: Admittedly, I am far from being an organized romantic—creativity is my strength. This is an idea I could have never written about, so thanks to Angela for sending it in.)

Christmas in July

Most people have a love–hate relationship with Christmas. They love the food, hate the weight gain. Love giving presents, hate the shopping crowds. Love the music, hate having six weeks of it. Love the true meaning, hate the commercialism that seems to overshadow it.

There is a way to have the best of Christmas and leave the rest behind. Celebrate it in July.

I'm not suggesting giving up the late-December festivities, but if your mate really loves Christmas, surprise them with a one-night bonus celebration in the middle of summer.

If possible, drag out the artificial tree while your love is away for the day or weekend and decorate it. If you always get a real one, go to a nursery and find a small potted evergreen to light up.

Bake some of your love's favorite holiday goodies. Put a few presents under the tree. Turn the air conditioner on high and light a crackling fire in the fireplace while listening to your favorite Christmas tunes.

Of course you can't forget the eggnog. Most stores don't carry it in the summer so you will have to make it from scratch. Here's one recipe:

    1 dozen medium eggs
    1 cup sugar
    1½ quarts milk
    1 pint heavy cream, whipped
    Up to 750 milliliters of brandy or rum, if desired
    Powdered nutmeg

Separate eggs, beat yolks in large serving bowl, adding sugar while beating. Stir in milk and cream. If using alcohol, slowly add and then refrigerate for at least 1 hour. Before serving, whip egg whites stiff. Mix into eggnog, dust with nutmeg.

Letterbox Love

Whether you are in a long-distance relationship or a short-distance one, communication is vital. One way to communicate is through the mail. And an inexpensive way to do so is with postcards.

Postcards only cost twenty cents to mail in the United States. Some restaurants, bookstores, or shops even carry racks with free postcards on them. A company called Max Racks (www.maxracks.com) began setting up these postcard racks as a means of advertising for their clients. Most of the postcards are clearly selling something, but, hey, they're free.

If you have eight postcards you can put one letter (I L O V E Y O U) on each card and mail them a few days apart. Of course you can write whatever phrase you want and even mix them up before you send them off.

So for less than two dollars you can let your sweetheart know just how much they mean to you—one letter at a time.

The Sweetest Hug and Kiss

Kelly Doyle
Medford Lakes, NJ

Here's a fun idea you might want to share. Go buy a bag of Hershey's kisses and hugs. Arrange them in the shape of a heart on a table, bed, the front steps, or anywhere you choose. Place a card in the middle that says something like this: "Thought you could use some hugs & kisses." Try this for your sweetheart; they will love it. This idea will work especially well for someone coming back from a trip or who has had an extremely stressful day.

Got Milk?

As I have mentioned several times before in the pages of this book, sometimes the gift isn't nearly as important as the way you give it.

I remember from my childhood how my six sisters and I would fight over the "prize" inside the cereal box. We would go to great lengths to make certain we got the prize, which was inevitably at the bottom of the box. Mom would have to go to even greater lengths to make certain we played fair. She outlawed opening the cereal box from the bottom, which was my favorite trick. She wouldn't even let us dig for the prize. She insisted that we pour just one bowl full of cereal and if it didn't come out on its own, then tough luck. Heaven forbid if we were caught sticking our hands in the box.

Eventually, I think my mom stopped buying cereal with prizes in it to cut down on the sibling squabbles. It sure has been a long time since I had a cereal toy. I kind of miss it.

As I write this, I am trying to think of a small present I could hide in the box of Athena's favorite cereal.

Even a small card tucked among the Fruit Loops would make anyone's day. Besides the card or gift, you could lace the cereal with candy hearts, Hershey's kisses or M&Ms for added pizzazz. I recall wishing that there were more colored marshmallows in each box of Lucky Charms. If someone surprised me with a box that was chock-full of green clovers, blue moons, yellow stars, and pink hearts, I would be in cereal heaven. Sometimes I also crave other childhood cereals such as Captain Crunch, Sugar Pops, and Boo Berry. I could go for a great big bowl right now.

Everyone has a cereal craving now and again. Do you know your sweetheart's cereal fantasy?

Adult Toy Stores

A few months ago, Athena and I were in Chicago visiting some friends. They took us to see some of the sites in the city. We went to the Museum of Art. We saw the lake. We walked around and saw some great architecture. When we were tired and a little hot, we thought we would duck into a store to cool off a bit. We went inside Hammacher Schlemmer.

Hammacher Schlemmer is similar to Brookstone and The Sharper Image—stores that have items that nobody really needs, but they are cool nonetheless.

We tested out all the neat gadgets and inventions this store carries. We tried the massage chairs and the foot massagers. We tested out the various hammocks and swings. We tinkered with the games, puzzles, and other expensive merchandise. We "played" inside for over an hour. It is probably the most memorable part of our Chicago weekend.

Just as kids love to roam through Toys "R" Us, this was a toy store for adults. Now, this is the kind of window shopping I can handle.

Jump-Start a Romantic Evening

Do you have a garage with an automatic door opener? Have I got a clever idea for you.

The next time you really want to surprise your husband/wife as they come home, go into the garage and tie a three-foot-long string onto the bottom handle of the garage door. On the other end of the string attach a card or lightweight (nonbreakable) gift. When they hit the opener, the card will magically rise from the floor to greet them as they arrive.

Now, if you would like to go over the top with this idea,

tie balloons, streamers, and other festive items to the bottom of the door too. You could even create a banner that would run the entire length of the garage if you were up to it.

I can't wait to buy a house with a garage just so I can try out this idea.

Oldies but Goodies

Athena and I visit a retirement home near our house every few weeks. Many of the residents do not have families living nearby and even those that do don't seem to get enough companionship.

I find that after Athena and I visit with our elderly friends, we find ourselves discussing topics that don't usually come to mind. We express our gratitude to each other for what we have—especially our families and friends that surround us daily. We see how important "people" are to us humans. We are not born to be solitary creatures. Just making these visits has brought us closer as we hear the residents' stories and they ask us to share ours.

These "old folks" thrive on conversation, stroking of their arms, and holding their hands. Those who receive few or no visitors quickly diminish in body and mind. Unfortunately many people learn too late the importance of talking, touching, and listening. I hope you won't be one of them.

Paint Yourself Green with Romance

Mary Furnas
Lincoln, NE

I need some help for my wonderful yet unromantic boyfriend, whom I love dearly in spite of his unromantic tendencies. Please *help*!

He has the notion that once he says it one time, he need never have to repeat himself in the love category ever again. On one occasion he programmed a beautiful CD arrangement of songs for me and played them while dancing with me in the living room. It was beautiful. When I asked recently if we could revisit some of the passion we experienced the first few weeks of our relationship, he said "I played all the songs I knew, just for you, I told you how much I love you, and I don't have any more ideas. Can't you remember those?" He was very sweet about it and really had *no clue* how the romantic things can make or break a relationship over time.

I *need* romance! He seriously believes that once he says it, he never should have to repeat it. Please give him some hints!!

I tried to explain to him that love is like an immunization process. You have to provide booster shots in order to receive the maximum long-term protection against the "enemy." The enemy can be many things, like germs and bacteria that might cause our children to get ill, and in the case of love, if we don't get immunized and give each other booster shots the enemy can be, for instance, work, tired feet, hurtful words, taking advantage of each other, and forgetting to touch and say kind, loving things to each other. (Since he's an ex-farmer, I used the example of immunization of cattle instead of children.)

Anyway, I hope you can rush an issue of your newsletter to him. And, if you can, better to disguise the newsletter as an antique farm equipment journal—that will get his attention. I've even thought about painting myself John Deere green!

Label Your Love

Are you dating an oenophile? No, that's not some sort of pervert. It is a lover of wine. The fermented grape fanatics are fairly educated about wine and enjoy going to wine tastings or vintners' dinners.

Wine tastings and dinners can be an expensive but extremely memorable date. However, I like to remind people that one doesn't have to spend a lot of money to be romantic.

If you have access to a computer, you can create a very special gift for the oenophile in your life. Buy a nice bottle of wine and before you give it to your sweetheart, design a personalized label that you can glue or tape over the other label.

First, you will want to examine several other wine labels and note some of the important information that is always included, like the name of the winery, the type of grapes used, etc. Almost any computer nowadays has a program that can create a realistic-looking wine label with relative ease.

The label can be silly, clever, poetic, sultry, or humorous.

Whether you surprise them with the bottle at a restaurant or over a candlelight dinner at home, the reaction will be the same—absolute joy.

Two-for-One Romance

I am always trying to find new "dates" to keep our relationship fun and exciting. Not only will this idea provide you with dozens of unique places to have a date, it will also save you a lot of money.

Nearly every major and even minor city has some sort of discount book. The Entertainment coupon books, offering two-for-one specials for lunch, dinner, and other attractions are sold in nearly one hundred cities around the world. Other discount books are put together by local chambers of commerce or civic groups as fundraisers.

When I opened up my book, not only did I find dozens of new restaurants I could try out with my wife, I discovered loads of other interesting places to go.

There are two different discount books for our city of 100,000 residents. The one I purchased this year has discounts for the planetarium, go-cart rides, paintball and laser tag games, miniature golf, the zoo, life and science museums, train rides, and other places that would make for a wonderful weekend or evening date.

If you live in a smaller town, but would like to have a romantic getaway to a nearby city one weekend, this book might just be your ticket. Often there are coupons for symphonies, ballets, plays, laser shows, and musicals too. There is a section in many books that gives half-price rooms at hotels across the country.

A weekend in the big city might cost half as much as you thought while being twice as romantic.

Magic Puffs

Nancy Grizzle
Norman, OK

I once dated a man who was attending college and was so broke he was forced to be creative! We spent a lot of time at a nearby park, talking about everything—making wishes and blowing the fluff off of dandelion puffs (my mother always told me your wish would come true if you could blow all the fluff off with one breath).

One day as I sat at my desk at work, he walked in with a pot full of dandelion puffs, all wrapped in florist foil. He had gone to a florist shop and purchased some kind of fixative and some foil, gone to the park, sprayed the dandelions, stuck them in some dirt, and wrapped the pot in foil. He included a card that said, "May all your dreams come true."

Although the relationship ended a couple of years later, I still remember that as one of the sweetest gestures—romantic because it was so personal and so exclusively "us"!

Creating a Cultural Calendar

No matter how small or large a city you live in, you are bound to hear people with the same complaint: "There is nothing to do here." When Athena and I moved from one of the largest cities in the U.S. to Raleigh, North Carolina, you would expect us to say the same thing. Hardly.

If one knows where to look and if one looks often enough, there is always something going on somewhere. When we moved here, Athena and I began keeping a "cultural calendar" since we were not yet familiar with all the festivals and events that were available.

When I read the Sunday paper and notice something interesting coming up, I cut it out and then put the details on our calendar. We do the same thing with the weekly entertainment papers we read. I asked to be put on the mailing list for the various museums and concert promoters in the area and they each send me a yearly calendar.

Often, some of the more interesting events can't afford a large advertisement (or don't even need to advertise) so it is important to take a look at the listings of upcoming events printed in the local paper. By writing down these events there is never an excuse of "there is nothing to do around here" and we don't miss the shows we really want to see.

There are probably ten times more events on our calendar than we would ever have the time to do. Like a Boy Scout, a good romantic is always prepared.

An Engaging Finale

John Macedo Jr.
Red Bank, NJ

I have a great little story that just took place over fourth of July weekend. It was one year for me and my gal on July third.

I had it all planned, right down to the box the ring came in. We have our fireworks show here in Red Bank, New Jersey, on the third so it was all going to be perfect right there. Her parents and grandma were invited over for a big barbecue.

I had the guy from the newspaper come over to the house to cover the story. They said it was an excellent angle for this year's fireworks front-page story.

I told her that he was a friend who was interested in buying a motorcycle and had nothing to do that night so I told him to come over, talk some about bikes, and go down to the river to watch the fireworks. She was cool with that.

So, here's the setting. Perfect weather—cool and clear. We are situated on a huge lawn, overlooking the river with about five hundred other people.

Her family and mine were sitting behind us in lawn chairs as we cuddled and enjoyed the works. They were all in on what I was going to do this evening . . . it was going to be grand!

After the fireworks were over, people were getting up to leave when overhead came this object out of the night sky. It was a plane that had an electronic marquee underneath it and there in the dark were two electronic eyes scanning the crowd below. A friend of mine flashed the plane with the house's floodlight and that's when the show had its grand finale. . . .

The plane circled around, then slowed its engines. The

eyes disappeared and on pulsed the message: DANA...
WILL...YOU...MARRY...ME?...I...LOVE...YOU...
JOHN, followed by a picture of a heart beating. At first I
think she missed seeing her name up there and didn't catch
on even with my first name on the end. Then the message
flashed again, except this time, the five hundred onlookers
chanted along in unison.

There was a brief silence as I knelt on one knee and as
the crowd circled around us with eyes wide open and cam-
eras ready.

I popped open the box only to reveal one more little
surprise. The box had a light inside it that lit up as the
surrounding crowd sounded out with an "Ahhh!"

I put the ring on her finger and told her, "I don't want
to be your boyfriend anymore, so will you marry me?" She
wrapped her arms around me, her body shaking, as she
kept saying, "Yes, yes, yes," in my ear while the crowd kept
asking, "What did she say, what did she say?" I turned
around and yelled upward, "She said yes!!!"

It was so incredible . . . as she stood there taking it all in
and people began coming up to us with congratulatory
handshakes and pats on the back, the guy from the press
told her, "By the way, my name is Erik. I am from the local
paper and I have no interest in motorcycles." She fell to the
ground and was totally blown away that this was going to
be on the front page of the paper the next day.

I hope this qualifies me as a romantic guy . . . wait till you
see what I am doing for the wedding ceremony next year!

Serving Your Most Important Customer

When I first ventured into the working world I landed
a job that required a great deal of customer service. There
were some valuable lessons I learned on the job that I now
use at home.

Those who work in customer service are taught that when a customer has a complaint, we should first listen to them. We are often tempted to try to solve their "problem" before we even hear them finish telling us why they are upset. If we listen to their whole story, sometimes that in itself satisfies them. They just needed to let off a little steam.

The second step in good customer service is to acknowledge the problem and to be genuinely sorry that everything did not go as expected. A simple yet sincere apology satisfies many situations.

Only after we have fully heard the complaint and have acknowledged their suffering can we truly offer some sort of compensation. In many cases if you ask a customer how they would like the situation remedied, they will offer a solution that is both very fair and will have them very satisfied.

The next time your mate comes to you with a complaint, don't butt in, but fully listen to them. Be understanding and express sympathy for their hurt feelings. Ask them how they would like to be compensated for their troubles. If you treat them like they are your number one customer they will remain loyal to you.

Resurrect Romance Week

Can you remember the last Valentine's Day? For most people that was the last time they even considered doing something romantic (I hope my readers are different). In most cases, the romantic gestures that day had something to do with Godiva, FTD, or Hallmark.

Valentine's Day has turned into a multibillion-dollar business. That was never its intent. So I created an anticommercialized holiday, Resurrect Romance Week (the second full week in August). It takes place yearly six months after Valentine's Day, but it lasts an entire week. The purpose of the week is to place the emphasis back on our hearts and off of our wallets. To designate just one day for romance seems bewildering to me, so I am hoping that people will make an effort to do something romantic each day for an entire week. I believe if people do that, they will see an amazing change in their relationship and will be more motivated to becoming a year-round romantic.

Just what do you do during Resurrect Romance Week? Start putting into practice what this book has been preaching. Start off with the little things: brushing her hair, warming up the bath towel in the dryer, giving hugs, and calling just to say you love her. Plan a picnic or an afternoon of flying kites. Make a sentimental gift or a special meal and dessert. But don't go out and buy her (or him) roses and chocolates. Romance is not about expensive gifts (that often have very little real or lasting value).

Go ahead and mark your calendars now. Begin planning on doing at least one romantic thing each day. If you get stuck for ideas, refer back to this book. There are hundreds of suggestions in here. But this is the most important advice I can give: Have fun!

it's the little things:

....

placing a soft kiss on the back of the neck

Just Say No to Fighting

When I went to junior high school I said "no" to drugs. When I went to the marriage altar I said "no" to fighting.

Nancy Reagan's "Just Say No" antidrug campaign was a huge success. Kids made a verbal commitment and took a mental stance to avoid drugs before they were even of the age to be tempted. When they were introduced to drugs, they knew they could "just say no" and not feel alone.

Drug use among school-age children plummeted in the 1980s and many have held up Nancy Reagan's program as the chief reason. People who decide how they are going to cross a bridge before they ever get to it have a much greater chance of not falling in the water.

Why can't we start a "Just Say No to Fighting" campaign? I'll admit, we are up against tough odds. It is perfectly acceptable (and often expected) in our modern culture for a husband and wife to fight. Many marriage and relationship counselors even encourage it in the name of "communication."

Yes, it is true. My wife and I have never had a fight, not in our 110-plus months of marriage. I don't intend on starting. I made a decision when I was dating Athena that I would never fight with her. I saw firsthand how the curse of fighting destroyed my parents' marriage.

Certainly there are times when emotions get wrinkled, and the natural inclination is to blow your top. I sometimes have to bite my tongue so I don't say something I would later regret (since when is self-control a bad thing?). Having a naturally calm personality has admittedly made it easier for me to think before I speak than it is for some people, but that shouldn't stop anyone from trying.

Unlike many relationship experts, I don't see fights or arguments as healthy. I just can't imagine how hurting my spouse with verbal and emotional barbs (yes, they do cause serious pain) could ever be encouraged under the guise of "opening up and sharing your feelings." Baloney! I don't need to raise my voice or throw dishes to say I disagree or to explain what I am feeling. Neither does anyone else.

We don't fall for the drug pusher's lies that "everyone's doing it" or "just a little bit won't hurt," and we shouldn't be so gullible as to accept the old wives' tale that everyone fights and that it is a healthy part of relationships.

Fighting is not harmless. It is addictive and if continued, it is likely to cause irreparable damage. It's time to get clean. Go and fight no more.

The Write Way to Celebrate the First Anniversary

Roy "Dee" King
Shawnee, OK

If I remember correctly, the gift to give on your first anniversary is paper. Before my wedding I decided to keep a journal of my thoughts, feelings, etc., for the first year of my marriage.

I found a hardback journal with one of those cute Kim Anderson black-and-white children's pictures on the cover.

I have tried to write something every day. Some days are more hectic than others but I do write at least three times a week. As I add more entries I have also started to cut out cute cartoons, sayings, etc., and tape them into the journal. I even bought some stickers and colored pens to sometimes spice up the pages. Even though I have eleven more months to go, I can't wait to give it to her. (Just in case she comes across the journal before our anniversary, I wrote a note on the first page asking her not to read any further, but to be patient—she'll get to read the whole thing in the future.)

Just so you don't think I'm a cheapskate, I'm also going to give her a gift certificate to Bath and Body Works (another paper gift to her *favorite* store).

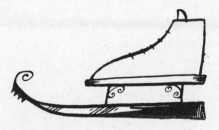

Skate Right into Her Heart

David McCord
Coppell, TX

Visit the local ice- or roller-skating rink before your Saturday afternoon or evening date and speak with the manager.

Explain your desire to surprise your loved one and make her feel special, and see if he will comply to clear the rink and have the two of you called out to skate-dance slowly to "your" song as others look on with gushing "oohs" and "ahhs" (and maybe even a little envy!).

I have actually done this, and you would be surprised to know how willing the manager will be!

Little Pieces of Paper—Treasure, Not Trash

Dr. Will Marling
New Albany, OH

I will toss in one of my little investments. I travel periodically, so I want to make sure my wife knows she is in my thoughts and I want to keep me in hers! On one occasion I used my computer to make a pageful of significant code words that we have. It is easy—just cut and paste the word over and over again. Then I printed it out on bright paper and cut each one out.

Just before I left for my trip, I put these little pieces of paper everywhere I could think of—in her cereal box, clothes, shoes, other boxes of food, etc. Not only did she find them when I was gone, she was finding then long after I got back. Then I would find them in my things. It has become a little game that has gone on ever since—finding these little slips of paper from each other.

Things even escalated! We now work to hide those little slips of paper so that they are revealed at interesting times, like when I open my notes during a presentation. Or when my wife opens her checkbook at the store.

All this over a little piece of paper? Hardly. All this because of love.

Removing the Barriers to Romance

When there are kids in the house both time and money can seem to be a barrier to romance. When you were dating and in the early years of your marriage the clock didn't seem to race as quickly and the paycheck seemed to go a lot farther. Now that you have children who take up much of your time and money, has the romance suffered?

If you have gotten this far in the book, you already realize that I do not subscribe to the notion that one has to spend a lot of money to be romantic. In fact, most of my ideas and suggestions take only pennies to execute. From growing up with six sisters and dating dozens of women before I married my wonderful wife, I know that most women are not interested in what's in a man's wallet. They want him to share what's in his heart and mind.

Since money is not an excuse for not being romantic, what about the lack of time? There are a couple of ways to address this problem. The first is the most common way and is how many couples have successfully kept romance alive in their marriage even when they had a house full of children. Establish a date night. Preferably this should be in the middle of the week when both of you are in real need of a breather (this is true for people without children too). If you can't afford a baby-sitter, try to make an arrangement with a neighbor or a family member with offspring where you can trade off watching the children one night a week. Invest in a pager or cellular phone if the children are old enough to stay home alone for a few hours. That way you won't be as nervous about leaving them on their own.

I know you probably think that you can't afford a night off during the week. There is always so much work to be done. Relationships need work and time too, and I think they should be near the top of your priority list!

Now that you have freed up an evening, how do you spend it? I think a good suggestion is to take turns planning your date night. You may want to set a budget for the whole month and either you can take four average-costing dates or two cheap dates and two more costly ones each month. You can plan the date in secret or give each other suggestions. Whatever works with your lifestyle is best.

Another way of freeing up some time is in the previous suggestion on rituals. You can take a small amount of time from each day and establish it as "private time" so the children grow up knowing and understanding that Mom and Dad need time alone to themselves just to talk.

Now that you have made up your mind to initiate date night into your schedule, what will be your first cheap date? Of course, I will give you some suggestions. That's my job.

- Stay at home and rent a movie, while eating homemade popcorn and snuggling on the sofa.
- Go to a coffeehouse and read poetry or silly short stories aloud to each other while you sip your coffee.
- Take your dinner to the park and then feed bread crusts to the ducks.
- Go to lovers' lane and smooch while listening to your favorite music.
- Buy one order of Chinese take-out. Make your own fried rice together. Eat in candlelight with chopsticks.

Soaking Up the Summer Sunshine

Ahh! The warmth of summer makes one want to play in the sun all day. When the ball of fire is out, we have to be outdoors to enjoy it, so we make trips to the beach, lake, mountains, or the country.

Athena grew up in Southern California and just loves the sun. If I weren't so overprotective of her, she would be driving a convertible with its top down on every sunny day. Every time a convertible passes by our car, her eyes open wide and I can tell she is wishing she was in that sporty vehicle instead of ours.

I am very protective of her, but I'm not a grouch, so I have rented convertibles for the days when we wanted to take in the fullness of the beautiful weather. They make a trip to the beach or mountains even more exciting and adventurous.

Another way of enjoying the magnificent weather together is with a tandem bike for two. There is no way you will get separated and you get a little workout to boot. With the bicycle you can even have a conversation unlike in a convertible, where you have to scream over the roaring wind that messes up your hair. For once, it doesn't matter if your hair gets messed up. Go soak up some sun together.

A Feather in Your Card

Have you ever sent your significant other a card in the mail? If so, you are to be commended. Would you like to add some variety and make sending a card explodingly romantic? Include a little something else in the card. Like what, you ask? For starters you can blow up a balloon, write a message with a permanent marker, give it a minute or two to dry, and then let the air out. Put the balloon in with the card. Here are a few other small but meaningful items you can send. Some have symbolic significance, others are just beautiful and are sure to ignite some passion.

♦ Feathers
♦ Matchbooks
♦ Interesting leaves
♦ A butterfly wing (please don't rip one off a living butterfly—that is utterly *un*romantic)
♦ Pressed flowers
♦ Packets of seeds

Stationery Is on the Move

Kinko's, the copy store with chains all across the U.S., has some rather useful products besides their copy machines.

The item that I purchased a few months ago was amazingly inexpensive and a great concept. Several places now sell stationery by the sheet (and envelope) instead of the box. There were about twelve designs that were appropriately "romantic" for my plan. There were designs with roses, flower gardens, jungles, teapots, luscious grapes, sunsets, and other scenes.

I bought one sheet of each design I liked—twelve in all. The entire purchase cost me about a dollar, rather cheap in my book. I put the stationery up with the rest of my romantic arsenal.

A few days ago I took them out. It was a day my wife had to travel out of town on a business meeting and luncheon (which means we didn't get to eat lunch together— sniff). I knew it would be a long day for her, so I wanted to welcome her home in a nice way.

I used my handy-dandy little computer to compose a different short saying in a unique font for each piece of stationery. For example, on the one with roses on it, I wrote, "God did create a rose without thorns—you." I took the pages and placed them in a trail from the front door and into my office where I would be working, putting this book together.

When she arrived home she ran up the stairs and gave me a big hug and wet kiss. I guess she liked it.

Once Upon a Time

Occasionally my wife will have insomnia and has a little difficulty getting to sleep. If I am not exhausted, I will sometimes tell her a fairy tale to help pass the time until she becomes a little drowsy.

You can read a fairy tale from children's books lying around the house. Personally, I like to make up my own. Of course she is the main character and I am usually her knight in shining armor who comes to save the day. Not only do the fairy tales help her fall asleep, they are wonderful ways for me to improve my creativity, storytelling, and extemporaneous speaking skills. I have to do a lot of thinking on my feet when reporters call me out of the blue and want to interview me on live radio.

Please don't make the fairy tale too gruesome, otherwise she might fall asleep and then have disturbing dreams. A good fairy tale will have villains (her mean boss or rude neighbor), heroes and heroines, interesting locations, and perhaps a good moral to the story. Sometimes I incorporate riddles into the stories to keep them interesting and clever. Jokes and puns liven up the fairy tale as well.

If you don't make up your own story, just put some interesting twists on the classics: *Red Riding Hood, The Three Little Pigs, Sleeping Beauty, Cinderella, Hansel & Gretel, Goldilocks and the Three Bears*, etc.

And they lived happily ever after.

Seven Magic Words

Language is powerful. It can build up fortresslike relationships, but it can also tear down even the most stable ones.

There are seven magical words, said frequently, that will go a long way in erecting the walls of a loving, secure relationship. These words can even repair damaged walls of the most battered relationships.

The words are simple, effective, and easy to remember. In fact, you already know them. The question is: Do you use them? Those words are: *please, thank you, you're welcome*, and *I'm sorry*.

Do you say things like:

♦ "Grab me a beer."
♦ "I don't want to go out tonight like we had planned."
♦ "Don't nag me. I'm busy."
♦ "Why can't you pick up after yourself?"

Consider saying it like this:

♦ "Would you please grab me a beer when you have a minute."
♦ "I'm sorry, but I'm not feeling well. Let's plan to go out another night."

- "I know I need to get that project done. I'm busy at the moment, but please remind me later."
- "Thank you for helping me clean up the house. It helps me out a lot and I do appreciate it."

The adage is true. It's not just what you say, it's also how you say it.

On Your Mark, Get Set . . .

There are stock car races and thoroughbred races, but I prefer leaf races.

One of my favorite ways to spend a Sunday afternoon is a picnic near a gurgling brook. After the wine, cheese, bagels, and strawberries I'm ready to head off to the races.

Athena and I each search for the perfect leaf, one that is light enough to float briskly along with the current and yet tough enough to survive the ravages of whirlpools and being tossed against boulders. If there are no leaves to be found, sticks can be substituted.

If you plan in advance you can spend a couple of dollars at the toy store and buy rubber ducks to race. Not only are these races wonderful for a couple, they are fun for the whole family.

What Weapons Are You Hiding?

I have lots of weapons in the house. My wife knows I have them but doesn't know exactly what ammo I have. She respects my privacy and doesn't ask any questions about it.

My romance arsenal is constantly changing. I don't want to tell you what is currently in it because Athena does read my manuscripts. I will give you some vague ideas about what I hide there.

Of course I have a revolving supply of cards and materials to make cards in my weapon box.

Occasionally there are Hershey's kisses or other chocolates which eventually find their way on to my wife's pillow, vanity, writing desk, or other special place.

In the past, I have hidden my glow-in-the-dark chalk and stars in my weapon box while I pondered how and when to best use them. My box has also been home to Rain-X antifog (see Mirror, Mirror on the Bathroom Wall on page 152), Silly String, and several other zany items.

Perhaps the target of your affection doesn't know you own this book. Maybe you hide it somewhere as a reference for future romantic "attacks." But do you have enough ammunition? Are you prepared for a surprise attack?

Start building up your supplies today. I really beef up my supplies after Valentine's each year when the items go on clearance. There are chocolates, stickers, unique candies, candles, small books, and many, many other items that you can stash away for emergencies.

Time for me to go use up some of my supplies.

The Four Seasons

Like the seasons, people change throughout the year. Women and men have a noticeable reaction to the climate outdoors and the changes in the seasons. It was probably this very reason many marriage counselors recommend this dating ritual: A relationship should be well-*seasoned* before there is a commitment to marriage. After witnessing dozens of courtships, engagements, marriages, and divorces, I firmly believe that a couple should date in the winter, spring, summer, and autumn before tying the knot.

It is a well-documented statistic that couples who have dated for a year or longer before marriage have a significantly lower rate of divorce than those who married after a short dating period. A year of dating gives time for many emotions to surface and many character traits to be discovered. You may adore someone in the spring, but despise them in the winter. Asking someone for their hand in marriage on the third date isn't romantic. It's gambling.

Store-Bought or Hand-Wrought?

Do you remember when you were a child and made a card or gift for your mother for her birthday, Mother's Day, or some other occasion? I fondly recall the joy I saw on my mom's face when I presented her with a jewelry box I made by gluing gold-spray-painted pasta shells on the outside of a painted cigar box. I don't think I could have bought her anything that would have made her more pleased.

A gift from the heart—and hands—will be treasured forever. It speaks of a pure love. Anyone can buy a present at the store, but it takes a greater effort to use your own hands and time to create something for the one you love.

A man doesn't have to be talented or creative by nature to produce a gift that will be adored by his wife. Five-year-olds rarely create true works of art but what they do make for their parents are priceless treasures.

The next time you are looking for a card or gift for your wife, why not consider a gift from your heart—and hands.

The Best of Both

Gary Lynn Corker
São Paulo Brazil

I was elected this past year to be the president of our church's men's ministry. Each quarter we have a meeting on Saturday night for inspiration and fellowship.

The last meeting was June 6 and in addition to the regular speaker I used your materials to share Twelve Suggestions for June 12 (Dia Dos Nomarados—Brazilian Valentine's Day).

Now I want to tell you my personal story. My wife gets the best of both cultures. She is Brazilian and I am American, but I try to remember to do something special on both Valentine's Day and Dia Dos Nomarados. Last June 12 I did the following:

My wife was working for a chemical plant in a neighboring city. On that morning she had given me a beautiful Santos Dumond pocketwatch. I already had plans for her surprise, but this only helped me complete the plans.

I went that morning to the open-air market and bought a dozen roses (about five dollars, so I have no excuse for not buying flowers), then when I finished giving my English classes that morning I went to a shopping center and bought some pastries that I knew she would like.

Just before it was time for her to leave work I gathered up her china teapot and cups, some tea, a small wooden table, and a hand-painted place mat. Then I went to the chemical plant.

I arrived just before quitting time and asked for an office boy to take her dozen roses in a vase I had given her the year before with the following note:

> The Dumond you gave me says it's time for tea.
> Why don't you stop work and come join me?

The plant has a beautiful lawn in front of the administrative offices with a giant cage with two parrots and two macaws. I prepared the table with the tea, pastries, and the china. She received the note and thought that I had just come to pick her up early. She had no idea what she was about to find.

I think she experienced the full range of emotions—joy, embarrassment, etc.—because at the time she arrived everyone was passing by to leave the plant and had seen what was going on. She blushed, she laughed, but she asked me if I brought my camera to take a picture. When she discovered that I didn't, she insisted that we return on Saturday and set it all up again just to take a picture. I think she liked it.

I was the talk of the plant and even the home office in São Paulo. The plant director told her that she could have June 12 off the next year. (I succeeded in changing the opinion of some that Americans are cold and unimaginative.)

Romance Is as Easy as Pie

Fall is such a romantic season. Strolls under the harvest moon. Dunking for apples. Watching the leaves turn to glorious shades of copper, burgundy, and flaming tangerine. But what I look forward to most each fall is pumpkin pie.

I heard a while back that the most exciting fragrance for men was not some expensive perfume, but the smell of pumpkin pie. I agree.

Of course I do look forward to eating the pie, but the whole ritual of making it can be nearly as rewarding (I did say "nearly"). First, you have to get yourself a pumpkin or two. Pumpkin out of the can just won't cut it. Then you carve it. No, not with some stupid monster face, but with hearts cut out all around or some other romantic design.

Then work with your sweetheart to make the pie together. I usually mix all the goop while my wife makes the crust. She makes the best crust in the whole world. Make some fresh hot chocolate while the pie is baking and maybe whip up a batch of fresh whipped cream.

When the pie is done, take it out of the oven to cool (and to fill the air with its aroma). Meanwhile, place a tall candle inside the pumpkin. Then turn off all the lights so the candle will reflect the cut-out hearts all over the room while you devour the pie with your best friend.

How to Spell Love

Here's another magnet idea for your refrigerator. Purchase a bag of magnetic children's letters (usually found in the toy department) and arrange them for a special greeting. We went over to a friend's apartment, where the woman of the house had spelled out "Joel is my hot man" on the refrigerator. I am sure it was a great boost to his ego.

There are only a couple of each letter so your vocabulary will be severely limited, but it will put your creative juices in overdrive as you try to arrange the letters to express your love.

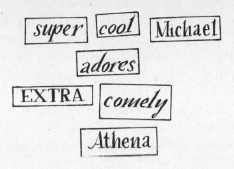

More Than Words

Finally. Athena went away for the weekend. It's not that I was getting tired of her—I just needed a few hours alone to create a special gift for her.

I'm sure most of you have seen the magnetic-poetry kits at gift shops. They contain a hundred or so individual words with magnetic backing that can be arranged to create refrigerator poetry. I think they're a great idea, but I wanted to make a set that was more personalized.

First I went to the office supply store and purchased a pack of twenty-five magnetic backs for business cards. They cost about five dollars. I measured the magnetic pieces and created the appropriate margins in my word processing program.

Then I began typing. I put in over two hundred poetry words like *stars*, *flicker*, *moonlight*, *touch*, and *gentle*. Then I added personalized words such as *Athena*, *Michael*, *travel*, *best*, *friend*, *sweetheart*, *cutest*, *girl*, and other nicknames and words that would have special meaning to the two of us. Of course I included liberal amounts of *a*, *an*, *the*, *I*, *and*, *but*, and suffixes and prefixes like *s*, *ed*, *pre*, *sub*, *extra*, *ly*, *ing* and so on.

I printed out all the words and then placed them on top of twenty of the magnets. Then I used clear shelving paper and placed it on top of the paper for a protective layer. I used a razor utility knife and scissors to cut the words apart.

Then I rummaged up a little box and put all the pieces inside. I created a label on the computer that said MORE THAN WORDS and put it on the box. It was ready to greet Athena when she came back from her trip.

By now, some of you are saying, "That sure does sound like a lot of work to me. I don't have any spare time to do anything like that." The whole project probably took me about three or four hours. It is true that you probably don't have the time in one sitting to create this. However, if you took ten to fifteen minutes of your lunch break every day, you could have it done in a couple of weeks.

If it still seems overwhelming for you, you can always buy the romance edition of the Magnetic Poetry at gift stores. It won't be personal, but it still is a nice gift.

Showing Thanks on Thanksgiving

I imagine that most of your Thanksgiving celebrations were similar to mine as you were growing up. All the ladies would be working in the kitchen, warming the rolls and putting the finishing touches on the rest of the dishes. Then they would set the table. Meanwhile, the men were gathered around the fire, working so hard to make certain it didn't go out or gathered around the television to "help out" their favorite football team.

The fabulous meal is then served and dessert is gobbled down. The men congregate once again in another part of the house and take a little nap or talk politics while the women clear the table, put the leftovers away, wash the dishes, and then tidy up the kitchen.

Wouldn't it be something if one Thanksgiving the roles

were reversed? The men would plan and prepare the whole meal to the best of their ability while the women enjoyed one another's company and actually got a rest from cooking for one day out of the year. Then the men would clear the table and wash the dishes while the women took a little stroll or catnapped. Now that would be a Thanksgiving the women would remember (and cherish) for the rest of their lives.

If the idea seems too overwhelming, how about at least doing the washing up or some other chore the women seem to get stuck with? What better way is there to show your thanks for all she does the other 364 days?

Blue Moods

Carlo Ingicco
Plantation, FL

I was away on business for a few days so I called the florist and had a small basket of "blue" flowers made up: white carnations, baby's breath, white roses, and anything else the florist could come up with that had blue flowers, would absorb blue-colored water, or could be dyed blue.

I then had this totally "blue" flower arrangement delivered with a note saying, "I'm blue without you."

From what my girlfriend said, and comments from women in the office, my blue basket was a great success.

You've Got to Charm Her

One predicament I get myself into is that when I am being romantic all year round, it becomes a little more difficult to make certain occasions extra special. This past May when I wanted to do something very nice for Athena, in honor of our eighth yearly wedding anniversary, I scratched my head and thought and thought.

Presto! It came together.

I found the box where Athena stores coins we have collected from our many travels. She has always been fascinated by the various designs, shapes, and colors of foreign money and would keep a few to take home.

I took about thirty of her precious francs, marks, crowns, pesos, shillings, and other coinage and whisked them away with me to the shed. One by one, I held them to the counter with a clamp. Out came the drill and each coin received a hole near its edge.

From my pocket I drew the sterling charm bracelet I had bought at the mall and the tiny rings I had purchased at the craft store. The rings are like miniature key rings. I threaded a ring through each coin and then attached the coins, one at a time, onto the bracelet.

Athena wears her bracelet everywhere—even when we are traveling. She doesn't even care if she has to take it off each time we go through the airport metal detectors.

The charm bracelet only cost twenty-five dollars to make. However, to Athena it's priceless.

More Charming Ideas

What gave me the idea of making a coin charm bracelet was remembering Athena's childhood charm bracelets she still wears from time to time.

Her charms are precious memories for her. A Tinkerbell she got at Disneyland, a San Francisco cable car, a mule from the Grand Canyon, and many, many others.

My mom has a charm bracelet that has children on it to represent each one of her babies.

A charm bracelet would make a sentimental wedding or first anniversary gift to your bride. You could add to it throughout the year or on each anniversary.

Here are some other examples of unique charm bracelets:

- Old lockets found at flea markets or thrift stores
- Bottle caps for a Coca-Cola collector or soda fan
- If your sweetheart is a board game pro, use Scrabble tiles spelling out her name

Wanna Be a Hero?

The other night Athena was getting sick from the paint fumes coming into our bedroom (she had painted the guest bathroom), so she went downstairs to sleep on the sofa. I grabbed a few blankets, my pillow, and a sheet and camped out by her feet in case she needed anything. I was her hero, just being there. I didn't even have to fight any dragons.

Breaking Open the Chains of Love

Sarah Watters
Oklahoma City, OK

My boyfriend (now fiancé) was going out of the country for a four-month overseas studies program. A couple of nights before he left, he made me a paper chain out of construction paper.

Each of the links had how many days he was gone and how many days until he returned. They also had sweet messages like: "I'm praying for you today," or "Think of me when you brush your hair." About fifteen times they said, "See (a specific friend) for a special surprise." When I would find that person, they would have a little gift for me. I opened the link at the moment when I missed him most.

I never opened one early. That chain made those hundred days so much easier.

Kissy Face

Lisa Moncure
Glen Allen, VA

My husband wakes up later than I, so prior to my leaving in the morning, I kissed him good-bye all over his face, of course with a lot of lipstick on.

When he rose to get ready for the day, he looked in the mirror and found ten lipstick kisses all over his face!

My husband got a kick out of it!

Three Hundred Sixty-Five Gifts in One

I like desk calendars—fun ones, that is.

For years I have been buying *The Far Side* desk calendar that has a cartoon for each day of the year. A few years ago when my wife and I were working for the same company, I used to send her my *Far Side* cartoon of the day (after the day was over). I would usually write a little note to her and send it in the intercompany mail. Often, some of the cartoons would remind me of something we did together or someone we knew and I would write about that. Sometimes it would be a little "thinking of you" note.

If you plan ahead now you can purchase one of the 365-day calendars for your spouse and write a note on each day before you give it to her. Have her promise that she will not look ahead. Remember to note special days on the calendar. It is really impressive if you can mention certain days that even she would have forgotten. Most people don't remember the anniversary of their first date or when they reach the halfway point to their next birthday. If you have any children, it would be nice to write a note thanking your wife on your child's birthday. After all, she went through a lot that day to bring you a bundle of joy.

You can use the calendar to tell your wife 365 reasons you love her or 365 things you want to do with her during your remaining years on earth. You can even mention 365 things you have done together in the past that have been memorable. It helps to look at scrapbooks or photo albums to jog your memory. I know it will take a bit of time to write on each day, but what other gift can you give that will be looked forward to all year long?

Create a National Holiday – Just for Fun

Allan Tobey
Grand Rapids, MI

When my wife and I were dating I "created" a national holiday. I told her a few days before our Saturday night date we were going to celebrate National Lumberjack's Day. It was fitting, since we lived in upper Michigan and it was the middle of winter. In order to properly celebrate this festive occasion I asked her to dress like a lumberjack: flannel shirt, suspenders, and work boots if she could. At the time she was attending a university and on the night of the date I arrived at her dorm room in my best flannel, jeans, and work boots, carrying two double-bladed axes, one for each of us. She was decked out in a red-and-black flannel shirt, black jeans, and winter boots. For dinner (we left the axes in the car) we went to the International House of Pancakes, because lumberjacks always eat flapjacks. While at dinner I told her that on National Lumberjack's Day all beautiful women receive a gift because lumberjacks never see women when they are in the woods. I handed her a gift-wrapped package. When she opened it she found an insulated undershirt.

She was very impressed with my creativity and the evening has become a very special memory we share.

Balloons That Will Not Go Bust

Mary Boardman
Des Moines, IA

A few years ago, I bought balloons in all shapes, sizes, and colors. I think there were hardly any balloons left in our city. Then I rented a hotel room and took the balloons with me. A friend and I worked all day blowing up the balloons. Once we had nearly filled the entire room, to the point where you could no longer walk around without having to push your way through balloons, we left for the day.

The next day, I had a message tied onto a balloon and delivered to my husband. In essence, the message said to show up at the hotel, room 21 (for twenty-one years of marriage). I went to the hotel that afternoon and blew up the last of the balloons. I had pushed my way through the balloons to the other side of the room, blew up the remaining balloons so the room was packed so full he could only get the door open a crack, just big enough to get himself through. Then the fun began as we chased each other through the balloons. We laughed so hard. It made for a memorable anniversary.

Crisp Rewards

Looking for a quick and easy way to reward your love
for all the special things they do for you? Make them some
low-fat Crisp Rice Treats (in a heart-shaped pan if you can
find one). Frost it with whatever flavor you wish. Then
decorate with M&Ms or other favorite candies. You could
spell out words or be creative with your decoration.

> 1 ¹/₂ tablespoons margarine
> 2 cups miniature marshmallows
> 3 cups crisp rice cereal

*Melt the margarine in a saucepan and then add the miniature
marshmallows until completely melted. Mix in the crisp rice cereal.
Put into a greased pan or form with your hands. No need to bake,
just let it form into the desired shape and serve.*

Mirror, Mirror on the Bathroom Wall

It's not that original, but it works. A little love note written
on the bathroom mirror is a wonderful way to start the day.

There are several ways to put a thoughtful message on the
bathroom mirror. You can write it with your finger on the
steamed-up mirror after you have taken your shower (that
means you have to take yours first). You can sneak into the
bathroom while she is in the shower and write a message.

I have used Rain-X antifog (found in the automotive section of most department stores) on the mirror, which works great for several days. You can squirt a little on a cotton swab and write or draw something on the mirror and the message will magically appear when the mirror fogs up.

If you can't steam up the bathroom mirror, there are other ways to leave a message. Try using an old tube of lipstick that your wife no longer uses or a bar of soap. Be warned, however, that even though she will be wildly impressed with the act of romance, she may make you clean the mirror later.

Picture-Perfect Present

I rarely find anything useful in junk mail, but the other day I came across something that I thought was a great idea. They were selling twelve-month calendars where you supplied the photographs for each month. You can probably order the same calendar through a local company that does film developing.

All you need to do is find twelve photographs of you and/or other members of your family that would make a nice picture when enlarged. It's fairly easy, not very expensive, and will make a great present that will be admired all year long.

When Studs Are Romantic

Alex Stenzler
Yorba Linda, CA

It was my girlfriend's birthday and I bought her diamond studs. She always tells me that she hates it when I buy her expensive gifts. So, I blew up a photo of her face to 5 × 7. I bought a shadow-box picture frame (there is a space between the glass and the photo) and I drilled holes through her ears in the photo. I mounted the studs in the ears and wrapped the frame. When she first opened it, she was pleased that I had only bought her a frame, but then she cried when she saw the earrings. She loves them and wears them all the time. It really caught her by surprise.

Should You Plan a Holiday Wedding?

By sheer luck, the day my wife and I were married happened to fall right before Memorial Day. Now we realize the true blessing of our anniversary date when we want to get away to celebrate it. Nearly every year, our anniversary falls on Memorial Day weekend or a day before or after it. That means we can go away for three or four days and not have to worry about using several vacation days to do so.

The only drawback is that many other people are traveling on that weekend too, but by planning ahead, we have never had problems with airline or hotel reservations. If you are planning a wedding in the future, you may want to consider getting married close to one these holidays so your anniversary will always fall on or near a long weekend:

♦ Martin Luther King Junior Day: Second Monday in January
♦ Presidents Day: Third Monday in February
♦ Memorial Day: Last Monday in May
♦ Labor Day: First Monday in September
♦ Thanksgiving Day: Fourth Thursday in November

The Most Important Gift to Your Children

One third or more adolescents report violence in dating relationships. Studies show violent teens often have seen parents battling. They just learn and model the aggression.—*USA Today*

Fathers, do you love your children? Do you *really* love your children? Would you like to know what is the single most important thing you can do for them that will increase their comfort, security, and happiness? Time? Unconditional love? A good education? Sage advice? All of these are important, but I consider one thing even more so. Love their mother! Really love their mother.

A child is protected and grown in the womb of its mother for nine months. After a child is born, it is cleaned and then immediately placed on its mother's bosom to be comforted by the unique rhythm of her heart that it recognizes from the womb. After that, many infants rely solely on their mother's milk for nourishment for a year or more. For the most part, mothers take on the majority of the responsibilities in protecting, bathing, and feeding their children in the first few formative years. A special bond is created between mother and child that can't quite be duplicated with children and their fathers.

Nothing contributes more to a child's sense of worth,

comfort, and security than seeing their mother well loved. Nothing helps children to have loving, stable, happy relationships than witnessing the same with their parents.

Children tend to mimic their parents' relationships unless a concerted effort is made not to do so. In my family experience, my mother and father divorced when all the children were still at home. Since then, each one of my sisters has experienced relationships with abusive (mentally, emotionally, and physically) boyfriends and husbands. Some of my sisters have commented to me that they didn't even realize that their relationships were abnormal. They were in the relationships that they expected. They thought that a relationship with a really loving man was simply fantasy and that no one really had those types of marriages. They grew up seeing their mother unloved and thought it was par for the course.

I would have probably ended up being a mentally/emotionally abusive husband had it not been painfully obvious what these men had done to my mother and sisters. I must state that my father was never physically abusive. He was guilty of being abusive on the grounds of emotional neglect. He was much more concerned about his own desires and expectations than the needs of my mother. He didn't realize that a woman needs to be frequently told and shown that she is special and loved. A woman needs to spend quality time alone with her husband, not just with the "girls." She needs a man who appreciates her special qualities and considers her brains more important than her body.

Until we men learn to really love our wives, our children will continue the cycle of unhappy marriages and broken families. Our daughters will be expecting to be abused, ignored, and demeaned by their husbands and our sons will neglect and damage their wives. If you really love your children, *really* love their mother.

Save the Poppies

In Australia there is a phrase: "the tall poppy syndrome." A lot of people are uncomfortable if one flower raises its head too far above the rest. They think it looks unnatural, so what do they do? They cut it down to the level of the other flowers.

Do you have the same habit with your loved ones? Some people have the hardest time letting others take some praise. If our coworker gets a promotion we tease him/her about what devious things he/she did to get it. If our brothers and sisters brought home better report cards, we discounted the difficulty of the classes they took. We find it hard to accept that some people are going to naturally rise above others. That person might even be a spouse who makes more money, has a better physique, more friends, or is better educated.

We also have this nasty habit of cutting down all the poppies around us if we are feeling particularly low about ourselves. I remember when my sister made a rude comment about my thinning hair so I launched back an equally unkind comment about her thickening waist. We could have acted more maturely and watered each other with kind comments and encouraging remarks, but ignorantly we were tearing up the flower garden so no one could enjoy its beauty.

Do you like to insult (talk trash, dis, cut, slice) others? Does it make you feel like your poppy has grown higher? My personal peeve is when spouses spout insults about each other in front of their friends. They think their clever but insulting remarks will make their flower look prettier but in reality your mate's flower is wrapped around yours. If you cut theirs down, yours will be butchered too. Whoever came up with the "sticks and stones" phrase wasn't very bright. Insults are verbal sticks and stones and they can tear up a field of beautiful poppies in no time.

Got It? Flaunt It

Athena and I love to have friends and family come stay with us. It is not unusual to have three different sets of visitors within a month's time. Do I hold back on the hugs and kisses when friends are in the same room with us? Hardly.

Growing up, I never saw any tenderness or affection expressed between any husband and wife in my family. I nearly fell into the same trap.

Years ago I would have severely limited my hugs and kisses in front of our company. Now I realize we need more public examples of romance, not less. I'm not talking about make-out sessions, but the gentle things you do to express your affection. Children, friends, and neighbors need to see more couples holding hands, exchanging butterfly kisses, and gazing into each other's eyes. It's how they are going to learn to be romantic themselves.

If you had a friend who needed some training in order to get a better job, would you show him a few tips? What if he needed to improve his marriage, would you be too embarrassed to show him how to be more loving?

It means a great deal to women to be publicly admired and cherished.

Don't be ashamed of your love, flaunt it. It may help more people than you can ever imagine.

Is There a Curious Spouse in the House?

Doug Dynes
Phoenix, AZ

This is an idea for the spouse with a curiosity. My wife loves to investigate gifts. She shakes them, smells them, anything to try to figure out what is inside!

Well, this turns out to be an opportunity for the fun-loving person. Last Christmas, I included some extra items when wrapping her gifts, but did take care not to damage or dirty the gift.

If you include some nuts and bolts inside a small container, it gives an excellent rattle sound. Adding a piece of wood or other object when wrapping eliminates the boring box shape. If you're really brave, you might try a bottle partially filled with water—imagine her surprise when the package sloshes!

Annual Autumn Outing

Karen Heinrich
Fort Mason, IA

Several years ago I had a job at which I worked Monday through noon on Saturday. My husband worked four ten-hour days. When I got off work each Saturday, I had to look forward to doing all my "weekend" work in the day and a half I had left while my husband had his chores done (and some of mine) and was looking forward to spending time with me. Neither of us was very happy about the situation.

One beautiful autumn Saturday, I arrived home to find my husband had a picnic packed. He even had prepared a small charcoal grill. The truck was loaded with the provisions, lounge chairs, and reading material.

My mate declared that we were taking the day off and were going to enjoy ourselves. We crossed the Mississippi River and found a beautiful picnic area on the river's edge. We spent the entire afternoon soaking up the sun's rays, reading (by ourselves and to each other), roasting marshmallows, and watching the river traffic.

I hate the thought of each oncoming winter, but one bright event is our now annual fall picnic by the river. We try to figure out the last weekend which will be warm enough. The housework and the leaf raking is forgotten and we spend the day enjoying nature and each other.

We celebrated our thirty-fourth anniversary this August. During those years, my husband has done many roMANtic things, but that surprise stands out as one of the best.

Hide It for a Rainy Day

There was a big thunderstorm in North Carolina the other morning and my wife decided to wear her raincoat to work—finally!

About six months ago I'd put a card in the pocket of the coat for her to find on one of those cold, miserable, rainy days. By the time she discovered the card, it was in the heat of summer, but the result was just as rewarding.

Because of the huge thunderstorm she was extremely busy and stressed that day (Athena was working at a power company then). She could not have discovered the card at a better time.

The bottle of aspirin is another perfect place to hide some kind words—especially if your mate is getting the pills for your crabby headache.

Does your sweetheart turn to literature when feeling a bit blue? Maybe he/she reads the Psalms or Proverbs from the Bible. A small note tucked between the pages of a favorite book is bound to be an even better pick-me-up than the book itself.

Any love note is good, but the impact is even stronger when hidden so it will be found when it is needed most.

Love Builds a House

It has been our tradition these last few years to create a gingerbread house for Thanksgiving.

The first year I got a bit carried away and decided to create a gingerbread mansion. It was a couple of stories high and had wings and high-pitched roofs. I designed it from scratch and made templates for all the wall pieces and roof pieces. I even added a couple of chimneys.

The second year I wised up and made something a bit

more traditional. In the end, Athena and I had more time for decorating the cottage with various candies so that it looked almost as impressive as the mansion I first built.

A couple of tips from one who has learned. Be sure to use a recipe that is created specifically for building (which is different than recipes for cookies and cake). Regardless, gingerbread does not cool in the exact shape you cut out. That is the reason why it is usually covered with icing—to hide all the imperfections. Have plenty of icing on hand, and it is best if you have four hands working on the house to assemble it.

Athena and I have a terrific time on our yearly project. We labor together making the dough, cutting out the pieces, and putting our masterpiece together. We listen to music and chat for hours as we place M&Ms on the roof and mints on the sides of the house.

This is one tradition I hope we continue until our hands are no longer able to hold steady. It fills our life with warmth, happiness, and a true sense of family. Perhaps the highlight of our experience is when the house is complete and we then share it with others.

One final tip. Hide a small gift inside the gingerbread house before you seal up the walls. It will be a great discovery when your love begins munching on the architectural delight.

Sleepless in Minnesota

Anonymous
MN

I don't know if this constitutes romance or not, but it is by far the most loving thing my husband has ever done for me. I think he would kill me if you printed our names, but

I want to tell the story even if I have to do so anonymously.

One weekend night this spring, a piece of my tooth broke off. The sharp edges were painful on my tongue and I couldn't get in to see a dentist until Monday morning. My tongue bled part of the night and I lay awake for the rest of it.

My husband took pity on me, found a nail file, and proceeded to file my tooth down—very slowly, ever so gently.

There we were at my bedside at 2:00 A.M., me with my mouth agape and him bent at an awkward angle trying to reach all the way into my mouth to get at that tooth, which was a molar way in the back. He had to file very hard to get the sharp edge down, but he did it and I was able to get some sleep.

I still chuckle to myself when I remember that midnight scene, but I know how lucky I am to have a spouse who will do something so outrageous, but so necessary, for me!

Thank the In-Laws

Do you like the way your wife is kind to strangers or is especially good with children? Does she have good posture and impeccable manners? Is she frugal with the family income and creates great meals? Are there any other attributes you especially appreciate in your wife? Whether you like it or not, your in-laws may have something to do with it.

Have you ever thanked your in-laws for some of the great qualities they instilled in your wife? Punctuality, politeness, a strong work ethic, honesty, neatness, and humility are just a few of the virtues her parents may have taught her. And it is time you thanked them for their part (no matter how small) in molding your wife into the person you love.

This exercise is particularly helpful if you don't have a close relationship with your in-laws. It may help smooth over any friction that has occurred between you and them.

All people (including in-laws) have at least one good quality. For you to let them know that you notice and appreciate that quality will go a long way in continuing a happy marriage with their daughter.

A good time to share this with them would be your wife's birthday or on your anniversary. Your wife's parents were instrumental in rearing and teaching their daughter since the day she was born, and each year on your anniversary you should remember all the wonderful qualities that made you want to marry her.

Put on a Happy Face

Bruce Martin
Anaheim, CA

My girlfriend was having a real bad day at work. So when she left I made a big happy face and tacked it to the ceiling of her office. I then left a note stating, "Things getting you down? Just look up." It went over great! Whenever she got down she would just look and smile. It stayed on her ceiling for over a year until the company moved.

Share the Sunday Section

I'm not very good at crossword puzzles. On my own I can usually fill out two thirds of it with a little bit of difficulty. However, when Athena and I work on one together it is much more fun and a lot less frustrating.

I know of couples where it is a weekly ritual to get the Sunday paper and work out the crossword puzzle together over coffee and pastries. Some of them have the paper delivered at home and others walk or drive to a café or donut shop and read the paper and complete the crossword puzzle there. If crossword puzzles are not your style, how about the Jumble puzzles or at least reading the comics to each other?

Tremendous satisfaction comes from tasks completed together. It binds a couple together. All too often he reads the sports section and she reads the home section and little is read together. Nothing is shared.

Begin a new tradition in your family to start the week off right: share the Sunday paper and maybe do a crossword puzzle together.

Two Truths and a Lie

A few ideas back I shared with you a game that helps you to get to know each other better (see The Question Game on page 65). Here is another one that I have played before.

I call it two truths and a lie and you can play it with one other person or with many. You simply state three facts about yourself. Two have to be true and one has to be a lie. The others have to guess which one is the lie.

I'll go first. I am an ordained minister. I was senior class president of my high school, and I've been to over thirty countries. Which one is false?

With this game you can learn some very interesting facts that wouldn't come up in your typical conversations. You might learn that someone used to teach ballet or won a gold medal in a statewide swim meet. I have discovered friends who play unique instruments and have had the most interesting childhood experiences.

The more we know about each other, the deeper our friendships and relationships can be.

Who Is Your Secret Admirer?

Most of us have had a secret admirer at some time in our lives. It was a great ego booster to know someone had a crush on you. While it shouldn't be any secret that you love your spouse, it would be an ego booster for her to know that you still have a "crush" on them.

Remember those love notes passed around in class, sometimes sent anonymously? Why not pen a secret-admirer note to your wife or husband. As long as it is in your handwriting it won't really be a secret, but I don't think any man or woman would want someone else sending anonymous love notes to their mate. Mail the note to them at work or place it somewhere in the house or car where they are certain to find it.

If you are able to arrange it, have the note direct your sweetheart to meet their "secret admirer" at a particular location and time for a rendezvous. It could be for lunch, a cocktail, a romantic weekend at a nearby hotel, a stroll through the park, or some other meeting place.

Keep the crush alive!

Puzzle of Love

Buck Rogers
NSW, Australia

One of the things I do on occasion is make my wife a simple jigsaw puzzle that communicates my love to her.

Here is how it works. I find a cardboard box and cut off one of the sides. Then I draw a simple jigsaw pattern onto the box. I try to make enough of a design for fifteen to twenty pieces.

Before I cut up the pieces I write one quality that I appreciate about her on each individual piece, i.e., "You're a great cook," "You're beautiful," etc.

Then I cut out all the pieces, put them in an envelope, and mail her my "puzzle of love."

I have found out that my wife is touched not only by the words that I've written but also the fact that I've taken the time to express it.

The Beverage of Choice

The fastest-growing beverage consumption is not coffee as many would guess. It is hot tea. Tea rooms are opening up across America at an astounding rate. This means that there are likely several tea rooms within driving distance of your home. What does this have to do with romance? "Taking tea" can be a wonderful and romantic way to spend a Saturday afternoon. No, you don't have to wear a top hat and drink tea with your pinkie extended. You do need to exhibit some manners though (which, by the way, most ladies consider to be the height of romance). Eating like a beast at a fancy establishment completely ruins any kind of romantic mood. If you were really trying to make the afternoon tea a romantic affair, you could put on your best suit and buy a nice hat and gloves for your sweetheart to wear. And don't forget to pull out her chair.

Living Happily Ever After

Do you want to give your wife a gift that will make her blush, laugh, and cry? Do you want to give her something that will make her think that you are the most wonderful man alive? If this idea doesn't do it, I don't know what will.

What woman wouldn't want to live a fairy-tale life? It is evident by the numbers of romance novels bought and read by women that their desire to fantasize about heroes and damsels, romantic interludes, castles, and riches is very real. You may not be able to provide all the physical items that would create a fairy-tale life, but you can create that life on paper and include you and your wife in it.

Write a fairy tale for your wife.

The tale doesn't have to be long. It doesn't have to be masterfully penned. It doesn't even need to be entirely original. What it does need: a hero (you), a damsel (your wife), a romantic setting (castles, beaches, and exotic countries are good places), and a happy ending. You can add other elements to your story, such as villains, magic, hidden treasure, secret gardens, and passionate kisses.

There are different ways to prepare the fairy tale. You can create it on your computer, using different fonts and sizes and computer graphics. You can write it with a marker on colored construction paper. You can add your own illustrations or cut some out from magazines. If you want to prolong the adventure, try sending it in installments and have her anxiously wait to see how the tale unwinds.

Do this and you will live happily ever after (at least on paper, but hopefully in real life too!).

Hooray for Habitual Hugs

In our modern culture, hugs and kisses are the backbone of any romantic relationship. I don't know any married couple who would say they had a fulfilling relationship if they didn't hug and kiss frequently. Would you (or your mate) like to receive more hugs and kisses?

I began thinking about this and it reminded me of a childhood game I would play with my sisters. Each time we spotted a Volkswagen Beetle on the road we would lightly hit the other person and yell, "Slug bug, no slug bugs back." After playing that game for many years in the back of our maroon Toyota Corolla station wagon, it became a habit. To this day I can't see a "Herbie" without thinking of lightly slugging someone.

I have a new habit now. Whenever I am stopped at a red light, I lean over and give Athena a light peck on the cheek while we are waiting for it to turn green. I guess I could start doing the same when we are at stop signs or if we spot a McDonald's or even a Volkswagen Beetle.

Some theories claim that you have to repeat an action seventeen days in a row before it will become a habit. In other words, being romantic takes much effort and concentration at first and if we repeat it *consistently*, after a while it will come more naturally.

Giving and receiving daily kisses and hugs are important but we must remember that hugs and kisses are *not* natural for many people. Turning them into a game may be the only way to teach some of us how to make those physical gestures a part of our daily routine.

Cooking for Love

Jeremy Pettit
New Haven, IN

I am not sure how romantic I am. I would like to think I have it in me. I do know that I'm not a great cook. I remember a time when I set out to prepare a nice candlelit dinner for my girlfriend.

I had it all planned out with the perfect candles, the kind that twist around and make dynamic, wax streaks when you burn them, and I headed off to the store for the rest of my ammunition.

Armed with my mother's copy of *One Dish Meals* by the editors of *Reader's Digest* (Hey, I'm a guy. We don't have cookbooks!), I picked out the perfect recipe, seafood risotto. I remember thinking to myself, Hey, we both like seafood, how hard could this be? I walked from aisle to aisle, filling the cart with all the ingredients I needed, like tomatoes, carrots, celery, red peppers, onions, asparagus, shrimp, and scallops. I even got a bottle of wine. I don't remember what my bill amounted to, but I remember feeling faint.

I got home and began my ordeal. I chopped the vegetables with a knife (cut myself twice . . .) and made a grand attempt at peeling the tomatoes, which I finally threw into the food processor, skin and all. I sauteed the scallops, garlic, and the shrimp and finally managed to prepare my surprise. I set the table, poured the wine, and once she arrived I lit the candles and we dined while listening to soft jazz by candlelight.

You know, I can't remember to this day if the food was good or not, but I remember her complimenting it. I also remember the look in her eyes and her gentle smile, which made it all worth it. Even the bandages on my fingers.

Romance on the Run

It is a cruel trick of nature how our bodies turn on us as we reach middle age. We tend to sag, expand, ache and tire. And then we complain about our bodies and perhaps our spouses' bodies.

Unfortunately, women's figures tend to change more dramatically than men's as they age and especially so after childbirth. I am generalizing here, but most women are more sensitive than men and are greatly affected by those changes. They deeply desire to stay in shape for themselves and for their husbands. I knew of one of my wife's girl-friends in particular who had problems keeping the weight off, especially since her husband didn't care to exercise and could eat practically anything he wanted and wouldn't gain an ounce. Apparently, her husband didn't care too much about her being overweight, but it was an obsession of hers and constantly brought down her self-esteem.

If any of us find ourselves in that situation, we should consider creating a fitness routine that we could do with our wives. It could be tennis, golf, swimming, aerobics, or whatever you would enjoy doing together. Even a walk together after dinner would be extremely beneficial. Not only would both of you be in better shape, you would spend more time together.

Also, if your wife has a particular weakness for certain foods, it would be kind of you not to indulge in them in front of her or to bring them home from the grocery store. Just because you don't have a weight problem (or even if you do), it doesn't mean you should eat half of a chocolate cake in front of her.

It is not uncommon for many men to demand that they eat red meat and potatoes every night for supper. If their wife desires to lose weight, it often means that she has to cook two different dinners—one for herself and one for the rest of the family. As many wives will attest, there is barely enough time to prepare one meal, let alone two. I am not advocating that one should have to eat carrot sticks and celery for supper, but merely to have understanding, compassion, and a little bit of flexibility in the meals that are expected. If it means so much to you to eat a certain type of meal each night, you might try learning to prepare it yourself.

Most important is your attitude toward your wife's weight. Many men feel that if they complain, ridicule, or embarrass their wives about their weight, it will come off easier and quicker. First, the majority of women do not respond positively to that sort of tactic and often the reverse will happen—they will actually gain weight. Secondly, there are many things we should try to change in this world. Your spouse's weight is just not one of them.

Domestic—Who, Me?

Carley McCullough
Sidney, NE

Poor, poor June Cleaver.

Well, that was the idea when I was a kid.

These days, women can have it all. That was the motto of the aerobicising, shoulder-padded, go-get-'em women of the eighties.

I was a girl then. Unlike my mom, I was asked what I

wanted to be when I grew up. I was expected to go to college. I was going to be an air force pilot, a doctor, and a famous singer. I did go to college and ended up being a writer. Not just any writer—an I-can-have-it-all, I'm-as-good-as (if not better than) -any-man writer. And most of all, an I-m-not-going-to-spend-my-life-ironing-some-man's-shirts, go-get-'em woman of the nineties.

As a kid, I watched my mom prepare meals for Dad's Super Bowl parties. I saw her in an endless shuttle between the kitchen and the living room. Refills, dirty dishes, another round of pigs in a blanket . . .

I watched her smile.

I watched her serve.

And I made a vow. I was not going to be like that. I was not going to be my husband's servant.

When I met Sam, the man who would be my husband, I remembered my vow. No cooking, no ironing, no serving.

I stuck to it. Until I was sick of restaurants.

Well, no harm in cooking once in a while, I thought. And I do make a mean dish of chicken fried rice.

So I made the meal, and started counting.

I kept score. It's OK if I cook, if I serve, as long as he does something in return.

That's how things went for a long time. I mopped the floor, Sam did the laundry. I did the dishes, he made the bed.

The entire time I was tallying chores on my imaginary chalkboard. He had no idea.

I finally gave up keeping score, though. Not that the extra points for getting me a cough drop at 4:00 A.M. and giving up Monday night football (his only TV request) for an intriguing victim-of-the-week movie were all too much to keep track of. The secret chalkboard was wiped clean because I was losing. His favors and chores far outweighed my meager deeds.

Now I cook more often and occasionally bring him a beer

at halftime. With dignity. Now I understand my mom wasn't serving, she was giving.

Looking back, I remember it was Dad who made the oatmeal and quizzed me on spelling words every morning before school. It was Dad who ran the bathwater. He mowed the lawn, took out the garbage, gave rides to soccer games.

I can mop without hearing the old power-woman slogans of my childhood.

I don't have to keep track, even though it is Sam who takes out the garbage, feeds the kitten, irons my shirts.

Grab Bag of Gift Ideas

Looking for inexpensive gift ideas for that someone special? Here are a few ideas from Nancy Twigg, editor of *Counting the Cost—A Newsletter for People Practicing the Art of Simple and Frugal Living* (see RoMANtic Resources on page 189 for ordering information).

- Using a camcorder, make a special videotape of your children or grandchildren. Have the kids sing songs and tell what they love most about Mommy or Granddad (or your mate).
- Put together a basket of snacks for the TV fanatic. Include gourmet popping corn, bags of pretzels, cans of nuts, etc.
- Buy an inexpensive picture frame. Personalize it with your favorite photo.
- Make two batches of your love's favorite cookies. Put one batch in a decorative tin to be enjoyed now. Freeze the others for a later time.
- For the coffee lover, buy a pound of gourmet coffee and add a decorative mug from a dollar store.
- Pick up several different bubble baths, bath oils, and body lotions from a dollar store. Arrange them in a nice basket or festive bag.

♦ Check out the bargain rack at your local bookstore. Find a book your sweetheart would like.

but not
as bEAutifuL
as You.

Not As Beautiful

I would dare say that the happiest relationships are probably the ones filled with the most compliments. Compliments are often just another way of saying "I love you" without verbalizing those exact three words.

Some of the people with the quickest wits have no problem seeing an opening to insult someone but are blind to the myriad opportunities to hurl some compliments. Let me share with you one way that I routinely compliment Athena.

When I say things such as: "That field of wild daisies sure is beautiful," "The stars are really bright tonight," "This satin is so soft," "Those baby squirrels are very cute," or "My ice cream is so yummy," I often follow the phrase with "But, of course they are not nearly as (beautiful, bright, soft, cute, or yummy) as you."

You'll be amazed at the dozens of opportunities you will

have each day with this method to elevate your sweetheart above all others.

Just be sure that you don't make comparisons on auto-pilot, otherwise you could get yourself into a lot of trouble after you comment, "This box sure is heavy" or "Whew, is this cheese smelly."

Having a Heavenly Meal

Dining on Cloud Nine. No, that's not some new restaurant on top of the Empire State Building or an in-flight meal. It is dining on a cloud.

We all know that clouds are just tiny droplets of moisture in the air. What you may not know is that it is so easy to create clouds in your own dining room. It just takes a little bit of warm water and a few pounds of dry ice.

To locate dry ice just look in the Yellow Pages under ice and you will probably find several suppliers. Five pounds of dry ice will last about one hour in a tub of warm water. The warmer the water and the more the block of ice is broken up, the more dense the cloud will become (and the more quickly it will dissolve).

If you are not going to be using the dry ice immediately, pack it in a cooler surrounded with ice or stash it in your freezer. Don't buy it more than a few hours in advance if possible.

With this trick up your sleeve, it is easy to transform your next dining occasion into a heavenly experience. As a fitting conclusion to your meal I suggest pudding in a cloud (of whipped cream).

PUDDING IN A CLOUD

Take two clear dishes or glasses (margarita glasses work very well), spread thick whipped cream about 1 inch deep all around the inside of the glass. Slowly pour your favorite flavor of chilled pudding in the dish, being careful not to move the whipped cream. When you are done the pudding will be "floating" in a cloud of cream.

To Be a Kid Again

Kids love to have fun and kids love Chuck E. Cheese, arcades, Putt Putt, and similar establishments. If you think life has become a bit too serious recently, toss your worries aside and act like a kid.

Now, if you go on a date to one of these places for children, you have to play the part. Don't just sit back and observe the kids running wild and having a blast—join in.

Buy your tokens and throw some skee balls, rack up tickets for worthless trinkets and shoot basketballs into hoops. Ride the kiddie rides, if there are no weight restrictions.

If that would be just a wee awkward for you, bring some kids and play along with them. If you don't have any, borrow some. I'm sure your nieces and nephews or some neighborhood kids would think you were the greatest if you brought them. But remember, the goal is for you to have some fun too.

If money is not a concern, you can always plan a couple of days in Walt Disney World—and don't spend all your time on Main Street. If you want to have a memorable time on a date, just act like a kid—kids sure know how to have fun.

Queen for a Day

Decades ago, there was a television show called *Queen for a Day*. A woman, typically under a lot of stress, was given the surprise of being named queen for a day. The scenario went something like this: maids would come and clean her house top to bottom, a limousine would pick her up and take her on a shopping trip, to a beauty salon, then out to dinner with her husband. And she felt like she was a queen for a day.

You don't need a camera crew and a lot of money to treat your wife to a queen-for-a-day episode. You can arrange for a friend or neighbor to take care of your children, if you have any. If you explain the situation, most ladies would be more than willing to help you out with the plan. If you can't afford to hire a professional maid for a day or half a day, try locating a teenager or someone else who would clean house for less money. Then take your wife some-where she would like to go, perhaps to the park or zoo. You could plan ahead and pack a picnic for the event and have it kept at a friend's house so she will not be suspicious at seeing picnic supplies in her refrigerator.

The queen-for-a-day plan works best if you are able to surprise her. But if you have to fill her in ahead of time to make certain she doesn't plan anything else for that day, just tell her as little as possible.

Most important is that you make her feel special and feel loved. Kind words, cards, small gifts, and your attention will go a long way in making her truly feel as though she is a queen for a day.

Who Is on Your Thank-You List?

I receive thank-you notes all the time from subscribers of my newsletter. They really make my day. I send thank-you notes all the time. To reporters, producers, editors, sub-scribers, friends, and family.

I don't send Athena thank-you notes nearly enough, and she is the one for whom I am most thankful.

I should thank her more often for picking up after me. For bringing me drinks and snacks when I am slaving away on the computer for long hours. For gently scratching my back as I fall asleep. For doing the laundry and never com-plaining about it. For never nagging me but always gently reminding me. For always knowing where I left my hat and keys. For looking so darn cute. For cleaning the bathrooms. For . . .

Time to go write a thank-you note.

Petal Power

This fall I planted some tulips for Athena. She just adores tulips.

She's in for a big surprise this coming spring. I didn't just plant the bulbs in any ordinary way. You know me better than that by now.

Instead of digging holes here and there, I placed them so they would spell out "I ♥ U" in the spring when they wake up from their hibernating state and rise to greet us with their charming smiles. They are planted right outside our kitchen bay window where Athena will be able to see my handiwork every morning. What a great way for her to begin the day.

Of course you aren't limited to using tulips and you aren't limited to the autumn either. You can arrange any flowers, bulbs, or shrubs you like to spell out whatever loving message you desire.

To Do

I like to-do lists. Most men do. We like to accomplish things and take note of what we have done.

Athena lovingly puts together to-do lists for me from time to time. It makes running errands much easier if I don't have to be worried about forgetting to pick up some milk or drop off some important documents. She's very organized. I am not.

Sometimes I will write myself a to-do list and set it someplace where Athena will likely see it.

Here's a sample:

♦ Fix breakfast for my beautiful wife
♦ Check the e-mail

- Call the printer
- Hug Athena
- Deposit checks
- Get paint at Home Depot
- Kiss Athena
- Have a cup of tea with my best friend
- Tell her how cute she is
- Do 3:00 P.M. radio interview
- Design new letterhead
- Write thank-you letters
- Caress Athena's hair

Anticipation Is Making Me Wait

Have you ever planned a special trip and bought a guidebook or video about the place you were going to visit and gotten excited by reading about or seeing pictures of where you were heading?

Daily reminders of an upcoming excursion can make one anxious and eager. Likewise, by sending reminders of a specially planned event to your sweetheart, you can multiply the anticipation and enjoyment of the occasion.

If the event is going to be more romantic in nature, then think of some romantic items to entice your love with. Roses and pieces of chocolate smell of romance. On each day about a week before the special date, deliver, mail, or hide a piece of chocolate or a single rose or other romantic gift.

If you are poetic, try writing a verse to go along with each daily gift. If poetry isn't your strength, then write a simple line about how you are looking forward to this special date or trip you have been planning.

On one particular date I wanted to make really special, I bought a dozen roses a week before. Six days before our

date, I put half a dozen roses on her desk with a note men-
tioning I was looking forward to the grand event in six
days. I did the same three days, two days, and one day prior
to the date.

A little hype can turn even the most average date into a
special occasion. However, one must be careful not to over-
hype an ordinary date. Otherwise, the date itself may be a
letdown.

If the nature of your trip or date is more for fun, send
something festive each day. If it is a birthday party in the
works, you could send a party hat one day, then birthday
candles and a noisemaker, and so on.

For those who like to plan mysterious evenings or get-
aways, try sending clues throughout the week. An event
that is planned well in advance could be promoted by offering weekly reminders beforehand.

Pamper Your Partner

Few of us can afford to go to a spa on a regular basis or
at all. But wouldn't most of us like to have the opportunity
to be pampered for an afternoon with such treatments?

Have you ever considered having a spa afternoon at
home? You don't need all sorts of fancy equipment, just a
little knowledge. A hot bath filled with salts, bubble bath,
or other choice ingredients can be nearly as rejuvenating as
a whirlpool. Check out a book at the library on massages
and with a little bit of lotion and practice you will be able
to loosen the kinks in your partner's back and shoulders.

I've heard of women who use mayonnaise to condition
their hair and avocados for face masks. If you don't have
those handy, there are specially made conditioners and face
masks you can purchase.

I know nothing about buffing and filing nails, but I am sure Athena could give me a quick lesson so I could give her a manicure or pedicure.

The one time I did go to a spa they had on soothing music and there was plenty of water, juice, and fresh fruit on hand.

Let's not forget that we guys need to unwind too, so if Athena wanted to give me an afternoon at the Webb Spa, I wouldn't complain.

Work Less, Love More

Time and time again, people tell me my ideas are wonderful but they can't be as romantic as I am because they don't have enough hours in the day.

I have the same amount of time given to me each day as everyone else. It's how I prioritize the time that might be different. Besides my relationship with my Creator, my time spent with Athena is most important to me. More important than my job. More important than the money I make. More important than exercise. More important than my friends or other family.

Athena and I made the decision a long time ago that we were not going to be keeping up with the proverbial

Joneses. We were not going to work more than we had to so we could have the latest fashions, the big electronic toys, and impressive cars. Instead, we were going to work less, learn how to spend less, and have more time with each other, with our friends, and for charitable work. Basically, we choose to enjoy life to the fullest.

When I worked in the corporate world I would choose an extra week of unpaid vacation over a new thirty-two-inch television or stereo. I don't want Athena to go out and get a full-time job just so we can live in a nicer house or have better furniture only then to have little time to really enjoy any of it.

I am not against nice items for those who can afford them and don't have to work insane hours to attain them. But I am slightly perplexed at those who work too many hours or have a long daily commute just so they can have "things," never realizing they are losing something that is even more valuable and precious.

Women Love to Be Carded

Leonard Nederveld
Lafayette, LA

My wife works and I do the grocery shopping. Each week I get a card and mail it to her at the office. The kicker is that I address it to "The Hot Body" or "The Foxy Babe" or some such thing as that. There is a lot of room for creativity here.

Fortunately, she works in a small office, and I make sure the receptionist announces that "The Foxy Babe" has some mail.

After she gets her card, she always tells me, "You're so bad." Sounds good to me.

Midnight Picnic

Linda Salazar, author of Parents in Love—
Reclaiming Intimacy After Your Child Is Born

It's 11:30 P.M. and I'm just getting home from a fifteen-hour workday. Dragging myself up the stairs, I notice my bedroom light is on. Oh no, I can't believe Jim is still awake.

All I want to do is fall into bed and pass out. Hesitantly, I enter the room. What I see terrifies me. Not only is he awake, but he's folding laundry! Now what do I do? I decide to stay calm, pretending I don't notice anything.

"Hi, honey, why are you awake and folding laundry at this hour?" (So much for not noticing.) Flashing his contagious smile, Jim says, "I'm waiting up for you because I wanted to spend some time together." Great, I think. Just what I need—a husband who wants to be with me after I've just worked fifteen hours. (The truth is, for the past week we've been like two minivans passing in the driveway.)

I walk over to Jim, give him a wifey kind of kiss, and make sure he knows how tired I am. Unfortunately for me, his sweetness instantly has me not only chatting with him, but helping him fold the laundry. (How dare he be so sweet.)

Next thing I know, he excuses himself from the room. Now that takes nerve. Here I stand, alone, amongst a bunch of unfolded sheets and pillowcases. Just as I'm about to toss the laundry aside in frustration, Jim comes back.

He's carrying a glass of water with no ice (the way I like it), a glass of club soda for himself, two napkins, and my favorite chocolate, chocolate-chip cookies. As I eye him suspiciously, Jim places the drinks and food on the floor and gently takes my hand to sit me down next to him. He looks tenderly into my bloodshot eyes and says, "I do miss us and thought a midnight picnic would be a nice way to catch up with our lives." I am so touched by my husband's love for me that I melt in his embrace.

For over an hour, we talk and laugh about our past week. My exhaustion turns into elation and I'm thankful I married this man and had a child with him.

The next morning, when the alarm screamed at 6:00 A.M., I wasn't the least bit tired. As a matter or fact, I slept more soundly in Jim's arms that night than I had in weeks.

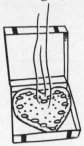

A Warm Heart Without Heartburn

Steve Casey
Shreveport, LA

Several months ago while I was "moonlighting" a few nights a week delivering Domino's pizza, I was able to be a part of a romantic moment for two young lovebirds. We received a call for a special heart-shaped pizza to be delivered to the caller's fiancée. Hand-tossed worked perfectly. Dawn, our manager, who made the special order, carefully shaped the dough into a large heart. Then the heart was outlined and decorated with pieces of pepperoni. It turned out to be quite a work of art.

I had the privilege of delivering the heartwarming creation. The young lady was so pleased that I was asked to hold the box open while handing it to the blushing bride-to-be as we all posed for a snapshot.

RoMANtic Resources

WEDDING DAYS Ever wonder which famous couples share your anniversary? Susan Gordon compiles 366 (with leap day) surprising, humorous, passionate, and romantic stories of how famous couples met and married, in her book *Wedding Days*. Great gift for newlyweds. At bookstores.

COUNTING THE COST Do you ever complain that you don't have the time or money to be more romantic? This monthly publication gives you lots of tips on simplifying your life and ways to spend less and save more. What would you do with an extra hour or two each day? Send $15 to:
Counting the Cost
Dept. TR
4770 Riverdale Rd, Suite 122
Memphis, TN 38141

SWEET TALK JAR This "jar" promotes communication through 120 thought-provoking and stimulating questions. Athena and I keep ours by our bed and we often discuss a few of the questions before going to sleep. Other quality products available too. $17.99. 800-771-MOMS.

ROMANTIC ADVENTURES This is a site just for ladies. Here you will find a few free items on romance and a secret-admirer package for women to use on their man. www.ru4romance.com

WEDDING 411 If you are planning a trip down the aisle in the future, this is one web site you might want to check out. It's like a Yellow Pages full of wedding information, addresses, and phone numbers. It also has a bridal registry. www.wedding411.com

ALL I NEED TO KNOW Do you want to know what women get out of reading romance novels? Millions of women (and some men) love to read about relationships gone right, and *All I Need to Know in Life I Learned from Romance Novels* shares some of the common traits in romance novels that *should* be in all of our relationships. At bookstores.

POETRY DAILY Poets are natural romantics because they are used to sharing their feelings or at least expressing them. This site features a new poem each day and other material on poetry. Perhaps it will inspire you. www.poems.com

LOVETYPES You are probably aware of the various tests you can take to determine what type of personality you have. *LoveTypes* by Dr. Alexander Avila helps you determine what is your romantic personality and, if you are looking for a mate, which romantic personalities you will find to be most compatible. A good investment. In bookstores or visit www.lovetype.com

SIGNATURE FACTORY The Signature Factory converts handwritten words into fonts that let you type your signature in your own handwriting. Personalized is always a big romantic plus. www.ngenious.com

TRAVEL THE NET There is so much travel information on the net it is unbelievable. Not only does this web site tell you about various vacation opportunities, it gives you many web sites where you can get even more information before you go. www.travelthenet.com

PARENTS IN LOVE Romance is often thrown out the window when a baby is brought into the home. Linda Salazar shows in her book some of the small but vital steps that parents can take to reclaim the intimacy after their child is born. Call 888-90-FAMILY.

THE LANGUAGE OF LOVE A look into the past might give you some inspiration for the future. Here are some codes of etiquette that defined nineteenth-century Victorian courtships. www.stormi.com/luv.html

BED & BREAKFAST CHANNEL This site includes listings of more than 20,000 B&Bs around the world. It lets you know which ones are offering specials or who might be hosting a mystery weekend or other special event. Sign up for a drawing for a free weekend getaway. www.bbchannel.com

OPPOSITE SIDES OF THE BED If the *Men Are from Mars, Women Are from Venus* book seems too voluminous, *Opposite Sides of the Bed* is a 150-pager that is the perfect book to give you the scoop on gender differences *and* it is easy to read. Author Cris Evatt doesn't simply fill the book with her opinions but weaves in thousands of examples and surveys researched from hundreds of sources. Very well done. At bookstores or call 800-685-9595 to order.

OFF THE BOOKSHELF I get dozens of romance novels sent to me each year. I don't read them and won't review them. There are other publications that do that. My purpose is to give you material that might help you with your relationship. One such book is *Anniversary—A Love Story*. It is written in novel format by Dr. Michael Adamse, a clinical psychologist. The story is about Richard and Laura, a couple calling it quits. Richard's mother suddenly dies of cancer and after the funeral his father gives him his mother's journal and a stack of letters his father wrote to his mother during their forty years of marriage. When he reads about the struggles and difficulties his parents overcame, his marital problems seem somewhat benign. An insightful look at relationships. At bookstores.

ROMANCING THE WEB The Internet is the perfect place to get creative ideas on romance. It could take a lot of time, however, to track down something of value with so much junk cluttering the www. Fortunately, there is someone who does all the legwork for you. Just sign up for their free weekly romance bulletin called *Love Letter* and they give you all sorts of places to go to on the web for ideas on gifts and other romantic novelties. Here's how to do it. Send an e-mail to: subscribe@me2u.com. In the body, type "subscribe LoveLetter your-real-name" (without the quotes). Or go to www.me2u.com and sign up there.

A NOVEL IDEA I came across a really interesting concept the other day. A husband and wife team have been creating personalized romance novels for eight years. They have written seven novels and with their computer system, they can personalize many of the details in the book so it becomes a book about you and your sweetheart. This isn't one of those books that will be read and then tossed away—it will be treasured for a lifetime. The cost is only $49.95. Order at www.yournovel.com or call 800-444-3356.

LOVE SWEETER LOVE There are hundreds of terrible or just plain boring relationship books in stores. It is a thrill when I finally discover a good one. Yesterday, I received a copy of Jann Mitchell's newest work, *Love Sweeter Love: Creating*

Relationships of Simplicity and Spirit. I read it in a few hours. That says a lot considering my short attention span.

Anyone who has ever dated, married, separated, divorced, or been widowed will find comfort and wisdom in these pages. Jann has a keen ability to share many emotionally rich stories and then boil them down to a simple, yet profound moral for us to remember and to apply in our own lives. If everyone followed Jann's sage advice about the simplicity and spirit of love, what a happy world we would have. At bookstores everywhere.

ROMANTIC QUESTIONS I came across a nifty book the other day called *Romantic Questions: Growing Closer Through Intimate Conversation.* It is a whole collection of topics from the outrageous to the sweet and the profound. If you aren't the talkative type, this is a perfect way for your partner to get to know more about you. In bookstores nationwide.

ROMANCE 101 One of the first web sites on romance and it is still one of the best. You can get lost in here for hours, reading people's ideas and stories on romance. www.rom101.com

LOVESTORIES.COM This is one of the very few "relationship" web sites I even bother to look at. Most are full of hot air, bad advice, or singles making fools of themselves. This one is a breath of fresh air and has lots of wonderful and touching stories on romance. www.lovestories.com

MARRIAGE MAGAZINE (FORMERLY MARRIAGE ENCOUNTER) This magazine is like the *Reader's Digest* version of relationship books. They include dozens of articles in each issue from some of the best books on the market. Six issues are only $19.95/yr. Call 800-MARRIAGE.

DANCE NAKED IN YOUR LIVING ROOM This small book by Rebecca Ruggles Radcliffe is a wonderful antidote for stress caused by the rat race world in which we live. It includes more than one hundred fun (another word for romantic) strategies to unwind, cool down, let off steam, and comfort yourself. At most bookstores or call 800-470-GROW.

TO KNOW YOU . . . BETTER I recently came across this wonderful game for couples. You move one space forward around the board for guessing how your mate would answer a particular question. You take one step back for a wrong guess. The strength in this game is the questions. They help you know more about your mate than you might ever think to ask. For example: Have you ever made a New Year's resolution that you kept (or almost kept)? The winner is taken on a special date by the loser (details are inside the box). *To Know You . . . Better* is available at bookstores, gift shops, or by calling 800-776-7662.

CUPID'S ARROW When flowers and cards just don't get the message across, "shoot" that special person. Call 727-587-9600 and they will create and ship a beautifully decorated Cupid's Arrow to you. It comes with a note and suction cups so you can attach the arrow to your sweetheart's car or bedroom window.

ROMANTIC SPARKS Do you have the desire and the ambition but are just plain awful at remembering dates or buying gifts? Here is a service for you. You can arrange to have themed and boxed gifts mailed directly to you throughout the year just before those special events (birthday, anniversary, etc.). Then you will have the unique gifts in hand when that day rolls around. Call 1-88-UR-ROMANTIC or visit their web site at www.romanticsparks.com

COMMUNICATION MIRACLES FOR COUPLES This small book gives simple and practical advice on solving problems, creating lasting love, and effectively changing undesirable behavior. It isn't full of the typical psychobabble. Available at most bookstores.

LOVE LETTERS—AN ANTHOLOGY OF PASSION This is perhaps the most beautiful book I have seen and would make an ideal present for the lady in your life. It not only gives examples of some of the best love letters of all times, it actually includes facsimiles of some of them inside envelopes glued into the book. The artwork is breathtaking. Available at most bookstores.

SPIRIT ON EMPTY? It's often very difficult to love someone when your spiritual gas tank is on empty and you simply don't feel much love yourself. You might consider attending a church or a small Bible study group if you aren't already. All of us need spiritual tune-ups now and again. Most of us need them weekly. Check out my church at www.wcg.org or find one that is equally warm and friendly. You won't regret it.

CREATIVE DOWNSCALING PRESS If you are looking to move from a two-income family to just one paycheck or simply want to spend less and save more, this resource is for you. For a catalog of their products, write to: *Creative Downscaling*, Dept. TR, P.O. Box 1884, Jonesboro, GA 30237 or visit www.creativedownscaling.com

TIME CAPSULES The time capsule gift set encourages men to give at least one "gift of time" to their wives each week of the year, and contains a heart-shaped bottle filled with fifty-two large gel caps. The set includes suggested "gifts of time" to put into the capsules or you can write your own. $29.95. Call 888-367-9949 or visit www.seemotivision.com.

DINNER DATES From shopping to dividing up the tasks required for assembling the menu, *Dinner Dates—A Cookbook for Couples Cooking Together* takes couples step by step through every stage of preparing delicious and elegant yet simple meals for two. At bookstores everywhere.

Index

Did any of these roMANtic ideas work for you?
I would love to hear your story.

Send mail to:

The RoMANtic's Guide
Attn: Reader Ideas
P.O. Box 1567
Cary, NC 27512-1567

or e-mail me at:

michael@TheRomantic.com

Submissions cannot be returned and become the
property of *The RoMANtic's Guide*.

Find more ideas at The RoMANtic's Guide official web
site at www.TheRomantic.com.